The Freedom Rides

Lucent Library of Black History

Anne Wallace Sharp

LUCENT BOOKS

A part of Gale, Cengage Learning

GALE
CENGAGE Learning·

Detroit • New York • San Francisco • New Haven, Conn • Waterville, Maine • London

GALE
CENGAGE Learning®

LIBRARY OF CONGRESS CATALOGING-IN-PUBLICATION DATA

Sharp, Anne Wallace.
  The freedom rides / by Anne Wallace Sharp.
    p. cm. -- (Lucent library of Black history)
  Includes bibliographical references and index.
  ISBN 978-1-4205-0732-4 (hardcover)
  1. Freedom Rides, 1961--Juvenile literature. 2. African Americans--Civil rights--Southern States--History--20th century--Juvenile literature. 3. Civil rights demonstrations--Southern States--History--20th century--Juvenile literature. 4. Civil rights movements--Southern States--History--20th century--Juvenile literature. 5. Southern States--Race relations--History--20th century--Juvenile literature. I. Title.
  E185.61.S525 2012
  323.1196'073075--dc23
                                        2011046549

Lucent Books
27500 Drake Rd.
Farmington Hills, MI 48331

ISBN-13: 978-1-4205-0732-4
ISBN-10: 1-4205-0732-X

Printed in the United States of America
1 2 3 4 5 6 7 16 15 14 13 12

Contents

Foreword

It has been more than 500 years since Africans were first brought to the New World in shackles, and over 140 years since slavery was formally abolished in the United States. Over 50 years have passed since the fallacy of "separate but equal" was obliterated in the American courts, and some 40 years since the watershed Civil Rights Act of 1964 guaranteed the rights and liberties of all Americans, especially those of color. Over time, these changes have become celebrated landmarks in American history. In the twenty-first century, African American men and women are politicians, judges, diplomats, professors, deans, doctors, artists, athletes, business owners, and home owners. For many, the scars of the past have melted away in the opportunities that have been found in contemporary society. Observers such as Peter N. Kirsanow, who sits on the U.S. Commission of Civil Rights, point to these accomplishments and conclude, "The growing black middle class may be viewed as proof that most of the civil rights battles have been won."

In spite of these legal victories, however, prejudice and inequality have persisted in American society. In 2003, African Americans comprised just 12 percent of the nation's population, yet accounted for 44 percent of its prison inmates and 24 percent of its poor. Racially motivated hate crimes continue to appear on the pages of major newspapers in many American cities. Furthermore, many African Americans still experience either overt or muted racism in their daily lives. A 1996 study undertaken by Professor Nancy Krieger of the Harvard School of Public Health, for example, found that 80 percent of the African American participants reported having experienced racial discrimination in one or more settings, including at work or school, applying for housing and medical care, from the police or in the courts, and on the street or in a public setting.

It is for these reasons that many believe the struggle for racial equality and justice is far from over. These episodes of discrimination threaten to shatter the illusion that America has completely overcome its racist past, causing many black Americans to become increasingly frustrated and confused. Scholar and writer Ellis Cose has described this splintered state in the following way: "I have done everything I was supposed to do. I have stayed out of trouble with the law, gone to the right schools, and worked myself nearly to death. What more do they want? Why in God's name won't they accept me as a full human being?" For Cose and others, the struggle for equality and justice has yet to be fully achieved.

In many subtle yet important ways the traumatic experiences of slavery and segregation continue to inform the way race is discussed and experienced in the twenty-first century. Indeed, it is possible that America will always grapple with the fallout from its distressing past. Ulric Haynes, dean of the Hofstra University School of Business has said, "Perhaps race will always matter, given the historical circumstances under which we came to this country." But studying this past and understanding how it contributes to present-day dialogues about race and history in America is a critical component of contemporary education. To this end, the Lucent Library of Black History offers a thorough look at the experiences that have shaped the black community and the American people as a whole. Annotated bibliographies provide readers with ideas for further research, while fully documented primary and secondary source quotations enhance the text. Each book in the series explores a different episode of black history; together they provide students with a wealth of information as well as launching points for further study and discussion.

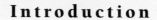

Introduction

A Fight for Integration

On May 4, 1961, thirteen men and women set out from Washington, D.C., to challenge segregation, or the separation of the races, on interstate bus transportation and in interstate transportation facilities. In both 1946 and 1960, the Supreme Court, in the cases of *Morgan v. Virginia* and *Boynton v. Virginia*, had ruled that such separation in interstate bus travel was unconstitutional. Despite these rulings, however, southern bus stations and buses refused to comply with the law. Blacks were still required to sit in the back of buses or stand in the aisle. They were also required to use separate restaurants and restroom facilities in interstate bus stations, as well as throughout the South. Determined to force the federal government to intervene and enforce the law, these thirteen individuals, calling themselves Freedom Riders, rode south.

The first ten days of their journey were largely uneventful, and the riders encountered only sporadic harassment and violence. That changed on Mother's Day, May 14, 1961, in Anniston, Alabama, when the riders were accosted by members of the Ku Klux Klan, a violent, racist hate group. After its tires were slashed by the Klan, the bus carrying the riders was stopped just outside Anniston by a growing mob of whites. Someone threw a firebomb through the bus window, and the bus immediately began to fill with thick, black smoke. As the smoke and flames spread inside the bus, the mob barricaded the bus doors, trapping the helpless riders inside. "Burn them alive,"[1] someone shouted. It was not until the bus's gas tank exploded and the crowd backed away that the riders were able to escape.

This incident was just the first of many acts of violence that were perpetrated against the Freedom Riders on their journey through the South. The initial riders, after being violently attacked in both Anniston and Birmingham, Alabama, decided to stop the rides. Other riders, determined to keep the rides going, replaced the original group; they too were attacked and eventually jailed. The rides, despite the violence and arrests, however, would continue throughout the summer of 1961 as additional riders joined the protest against interstate bus segregation. Four hundred and thirty-six individuals on sixty different buses would eventually participate in the Freedom Rides.

As they traveled together in small, interracial groups, the riders knew that their determination to challenge their constitutional right to travel would be tested. Whether through sitting where they pleased on buses or demanding access to all-white restaurants and restrooms in bus terminals, they also knew they would probably encounter violence. The riders willingly risked their lives in order to show the nation what the inequality of segregation looked like and to force the federal government to respond.

Giving African Americans a Voice

Bob Filner, who is now a member of the U.S. Congress representing California, joined the Freedom Rides in Alabama. At the time, he was a student at Cornell University. National Public Radio commentator Michel Martin asked Filner in 2011 why he joined the rides when he knew that he could be killed. Filner responded: "It was too important. . . . I had been brought up being taught that racism was the worst evil and you had some personal responsibility to deal with it. We thought we had to put our lives on the line, our bodies on the line, to make America live up to its ideals."[2] In the end, the riders' need to fight for racial equality was stronger than the fear of losing their own lives.

Pictured here, seated, are the thirteen African Americans who embarked on the first Freedom Ride from Washington, D.C., on May 4, 1961. They challenged segregation of the races on interstate buses.

The Freedom Riders gave African Americans a voice, a voice that would never again be silenced. The rides also provided momentum for the larger civil rights movement, which was still in its infancy. Journalist Roger Wilkins elaborates: "The idealism, faith, ingenuity, and incredible courage of a relatively small group of Americans—both black and white—lit a fuse in 1961 that drew a reluctant federal government into the struggle—and also enlarged, energized and solidified the hitherto fragmented civil rights movement."[3]

The Freedom Rides also shone a spotlight on the discriminatory and racist practices of the South and helped gain support for the broader civil rights movement taking place throughout the United States and the world. Civil rights leader Martin Luther King Jr. elaborated on the Freedom Riders in his autobiography: "The Freedom Ride movement came into being to reveal the indignities and the injustices which Negro people faced as they attempted to do the simple thing of traveling through the South as interstate passengers. . . . The Freedom Rides, which were begun by the young, grew to such proportion that they eventually encompassed people of all ages."[4]

These Freedom Riders were, in fact, the instigators of a movement that would eventually change the way of life in the South. On May 4, 2011, many of the Freedom Riders were part of talk show host Oprah Winfrey's television show that celebrated the fiftieth anniversary of the beginning of the Freedom Rides. One hundred and seventy-eight former Freedom Riders appeared on the show. As Winfrey explained the Freedom Rides and introduced the people who sat in the audience, she stated: "I stand among heroes. . . . If not for these American heroes, this country would be a very different place right now . . . and millions of lives . . . would be dramatically different."[5]

Chapter One

The Jim Crow South

Slavery had been part of American life for several hundred years when the end of the Civil War in 1865 brought freedom to approximately 4 million African Americans in the South. Promised full civil rights, blacks looked to the future with hope.

Those dreams were shattered twelve years later when federal troops were withdrawn from the South. Freed of federal intervention, southern state governments immediately passed laws eliminating black civil rights, which ended any chance of full equality for African Americans. A new era of discrimination against blacks ensued, as well as an era of violence. Historian Roger Wilkins elaborates: "Outraged at blacks participating in politics, serving in high office, and participating in law enforcement, the white South struck back with a vengeance. A reign of terror ensued, carried out by such vigilante groups as the Ku Klux Klan and the Knights of the White Camelia."[6]

All power—economic, social, and political—returned to the control of white southerners, whose main goal was to keep blacks in a position of inferior or second-class citizenship. The belief in white supremacy was deeply embedded in the culture of the South. Many southerners and other Americans believed that African Americans were inferior to whites. The prevailing mindset at the time was that if economic oppression and other

From the post-Reconstruction era to the civil rights era of the 1960s, the Ku Klux Klan used vigilante tactics to intimidate, attack, and lynch African Americans, spreading a reign of terror throughout the South.

measures did not work to keep blacks in an inferior position, then violence was an acceptable way of maintaining racial inequality.

Separate but Equal

One of the new discriminatory laws passed in the South was a law in Louisiana that required blacks to sit in separate railroad cars. Laws like this one, which required separate facilities or accommodations for blacks and whites, were known as segregation laws. While whites rode in luxury, African Americans were relegated to dingy, cigarette- and cigar-smoke-filled cars. The 1890 Louisiana law was challenged by a young black man named Homer Adolph Plessy, who, after sitting in the whites-only section of a train, was thrown off the railway car and arrested for violating the segregation laws. Plessy stated that he had been denied his rights under the Fourteenth Amendment of the U.S. Constitution that had been passed in 1868, granting African Americans full citizenship and equal rights.

After a Louisiana court found Plessy guilty, the young man appealed the decision to the U.S. Supreme Court. The case, *Plessy v. Ferguson*, was decided in 1896. The court, with one dissenting vote, ruled that Plessy had no right to ride in a car reserved for whites. Justice Henry Billings Brown wrote the majority opinion for the court: "The object of the Fourteenth Amendment was undoubtedly to enforce the absolute equality of the two races before the law, but in the nature of things it could not have been intended to abolish distinctions based upon color, or to enforce social, as distinguished from political equality, or a commingling of the two races upon terms unsatisfactory to either."[7]

With those words, the Supreme Court gave legality to segregation. As long as separate facilities on trains and other public venues were provided, said the court, and as long as those facilities were equal to those of whites, segregation was deemed to be constitutional. "Separate but equal" became the law of the land, and southern state governments did provide separate facilities, though they refused to give blacks genuinely equal facilities or resources.

Jim Crow

The laws in the South that mandated segregation were called Jim Crow laws. The name *Jim Crow* was first used in the 1830s when a white minstrel performer applied black face (or paint) to his face and played an obedient and uncomplaining black character named Jim Crow. The label was then applied to all blacks and became a term used throughout the United States to denigrate African Americans.

During the last decades of the nineteenth century and the first half of the twentieth century, the term *Jim Crow* was also used to refer to a series of laws and customs that were designed to keep African Americans in an inferior position. These laws mandated separate facilities for blacks and whites. These facilities included hospitals, restaurants, movie theaters, telephone booths, courtrooms, playgrounds, cemeteries, schools, and other venues. Professor Vernellia R. Randall adds: "The most common types of laws forbade intermarriage and ordered business owners and public institutions to keep their black and white clientele separated."[8]

Signs that indicated "Whites Only" and "Colored" soon appeared everywhere in the South. Blacks had to use separate, often dirty, restrooms, drink at separate water fountains, and even read at separate library tables. In addition, courthouses used different Bibles to swear in blacks and whites. Juries were all white, as were judges, sheriffs, and all government officials.

All blacks learned at an early age that they must comply with Jim Crow laws or suffer possibly violent consequences that could include beatings or death. African Americans quickly learned that they always had to defer to white people. If a white approached on a sidewalk, for instance, a black was expected to step aside.

Jim Crow laws mandated separate facilities for blacks and whites, including water fountains, restaurants, restrooms, schools, and prisons. Black facilities were always inferior to those of whites.

The Growth of Civil Rights Organizations

The first half of the twentieth century saw the growth of two organizations dedicated to achieving equality and civil rights for African Americans. These organizations, however, differed in the methods they used to achieve that equality.

The National Association for the Advancement of Colored People (NAACP), founded in 1909, was the first civil rights organization. The founders were a group of businesspeople, philanthropists, and educators, both black and white. Throughout its early history the organization advocated the use of legal and political solutions to achieve equality for black Americans. The NAACP would later achieve noteworthy victories in several Supreme Court cases that advanced the rights of African Americans in both transportation and public education.

The Congress of Racial Equality (CORE), another civil rights organization, was founded in 1942. The purpose of the organization was to fight for equality through nonviolent actions. The group was deeply influenced by Mohandas Gandhi of India and his teachings of nonviolent resistance. With a racially diverse membership, CORE staged restaurant sit-ins in Chicago in the early 1940s that were successful in integrating a number of northern facilities. It sponsored the 1947 Journey of Reconciliation to test segregation in interstate bus travel, as well as the later Freedom Rides. CORE today gives support to black economic development and community self-determination.

There were also rules about addressing whites as either "sir" or "boss," while whites could address blacks as "boy" or by their first name. In every social situation, blacks were treated as inferior.

African American Challenges to Segregation in Travel

While all the Jim Crow laws infuriated blacks, one of the most hated was the one that segregated travel. Historian Raymond Arsenault explains: "All across the South segregated buses, trains, and streetcars provided blacks with a daily reminder of their second-class status. As early as 1908 a regional survey of the 'color line' by the journalist Ray Stannard Baker had revealed that no other point of race contact is so much and so bitterly discussed among Negroes as the Jim Crow car."[9] Diane Nash, a young black woman who would later play a prominent role in the Freedom Rides, agrees: "Travel in the segregated South for black people was very humiliating. . . . [Segregation said] that blacks were so sub-human and so inferior that we could not even use public facilities that white people used."[10]

Since the late nineteenth century, blacks had protested such segregation by occasionally sitting in white sections of railway cars and streetcars. The Louisville, Kentucky, ride-in campaign of 1871, for instance, received so much national attention that the city of Louisville changed its law, permitting the horse-drawn streetcars to have mixed seating. Sojourner Truth, an outspoken opponent of slavery and a women's rights activist, was reportedly hit by a train conductor for refusing to give up a good seat. She sued the train company, which resulted in the conductor being fired.

One of the most troubling incidents on a bus involved the brutal beating of Isaac Woodward in February 1946. Woodward, a recently discharged black veteran, was returning to North Carolina from his Georgia military base. He was arrested in Batesburg, South Carolina, for violating the Jim Crow law that required separate seating for blacks in public transportation. Woodward was dragged from the bus and beaten by Batesburg police chief Linwood Shull and a deputy. The twenty-seven-year-old suffered severe injuries and was blinded in both eyes. Despite a federal indictment against Shull, the sheriff was found not guilty in a South Carolina courtroom.

Morgan v. Virginia

Another incident involving segregated transportation occurred in the early 1940s. An African American woman named Irene Morgan was riding a crowded Greyhound bus from Hayes, Virginia, to Baltimore, Maryland, when a white couple boarded and demanded her seat. She refused to move and was arrested for violating the segregation laws of Virginia. Morgan responded to the arrest by stating: "I didn't do anything wrong. I'd paid for my seat."[11]

Morgan was found guilty in a Virginia court of not complying with the state's segregation laws. She was approached by members of the National Association for the Advancement of Colored

The offices of the National Association for the Advancement of Colored People (NAACP). NAACP lawyers argued and won the *Morgan v. Commonwealth of Virginia* case before the U.S. Supreme Court, which found that segregated interstate travel violated the U.S. Constitution.

People (NAACP) legal team, who had been looking for a case that could be used to challenge segregation in interstate travel. The NAACP, which was founded in 1909, advocated the use of legal and political solutions to achieve equality for black Americans. The NAACP legal team immediately took Morgan's case and appealed it to the U.S. Supreme Court. On June 3, 1946, in the case of *Morgan v. Commonwealth of Virginia*, the Supreme Court ruled that segregated interstate travel violated the U.S. Constitution.

James Farmer

James Leonard Farmer Jr. was born in Marshall, Texas, in 1920. His father was the son of a slave and is believed to have been the first African American from Texas to earn a doctoral degree. With his father a college professor and his mother a teacher, Farmer took education seriously. He entered college when he was fourteen, hoping to become a minister.

During World War II, Farmer became a conscientious objector, stating that his religion forbade him to participate in warlike activities. He became a devout follower of Mohandas Gandhi and adopted Gandhi's techniques of nonviolent protest. He went to work for the pacifist organization the Fellowship of Reconciliation in the early 1940s as their race relations secretary. Farmer, as the national director of the Congress of Racial Equality (CORE), was instrumental in both the Journey of Reconciliation and the Freedom Rides.

Following the passage of the Civil Rights Act in 1964, Farmer remained active in CORE, turning his attention to black illiteracy and unemployment. He would later receive the Presidential Medal of Freedom, the highest civilian award in the United States, from President Bill Clinton. Upon Farmer's death in 1999, the Reverend Joseph Lowery, former head of the Southern Christian Leadership Conference, stated: "He was an authentic activist, willing to challenge obscene laws and unfair customs through nonviolent direct action."

Quoted in *Los Angeles Daily News*. "James Farmer, Activist: Champion of Civil Rights, Nonviolence." July 10, 1999.

Civil rights advocate James L. Farmer, an adherent of Mohandas Gandhi's philosophy of nonviolent protest, was the national director of CORE in the 1960s.

Despite this ruling, however, the law requiring integrated interstate travel was not enforced. Southern bus carriers managed to avoid compliance with the decision by passing segregation rules of their own and claiming that federal laws did not apply to private companies.

Journey of Reconciliation

After the *Morgan* case, James Farmer and Bayard Rustin of the Congress of Racial Equality (CORE) decided to test compliance with the Supreme Court ruling. CORE was a civil rights organization founded in 1942 as an offshoot of the pacifist organization the Fellowship of Reconciliation (FOR). CORE advocated direct action forms of protest using nonviolent techniques. The organization had had great success in the early 1940s in integrating public facilities in the North.

Farmer and Rustin hoped to have the same success with interstate travel. The two men, with the support of CORE and FOR, organized the Journey of Reconciliation—a bus trip through the upper South and the first unofficial freedom ride. They decided to limit their journey to the upper South, which presented less danger than the more violent states of Alabama and Mississippi, part of the Deep South, where racism and lynching were more deeply ingrained.

In early April 1947 training began for the eight white men and eight black men who would travel south. During two days of training, the travelers were given instructions on nonviolent tactics. They were taught not to respond to violence with more violence, to turn the other cheek when verbally or physically attacked, and to protect their bodies by taking defensive positions.

Taking two buses and accompanied by two black journalists, the white riders rode in the black section at the back of the bus, while the blacks rode up front. When they left Washington, D.C., on April 9, 1947, they were told that if the driver asked them to move to their designated section of the bus, they were to respond that, according to the Supreme Court, they had the constitutional right to sit anywhere they wanted.

In some cities the riders were greeted warmly by African American church communities; in other places the reception was lukewarm at best. White hecklers were present at nearly every stop, but

Passengers board segregated buses in a Louisville, Kentucky, Greyhound station in 1943. Within a few years, the Supreme Court ruling in the *Morgan* case would declare the practice unconstitutional.

Nonviolent Protest:
An Historical Perspective

During the Journey of Reconciliation, the Montgomery bus boycott, and the later sit-ins and Freedom Rides, the primary tactic used by African Americans was that of nonviolent protest. This tactic was an old one; it was used during the American Revolution when colonists decided to boycott British imports and dumped tons of tea into the Boston Harbor. The justification for nonviolent protest was explained by noted author Henry David Thoreau in 1849: "It is morally justifiable to peacefully resist unjust laws."[1]

Nonviolent protest was brought to the world's attention years later by Mohandas Gandhi of India. Gandhi's plan of protest led to a seven-year struggle in which thousands of Indians were jailed or shot by British authorities who were reluctant to grant the country its independence. The long protest, however, eventually led to Indian independence from Great Britain.

Journalist Anthony Parel explains Gandhi's tactics: "Gandhian nonviolence (*ahisma*) is an active civic virtue that habitually disposes individuals, social groups, and political authorities to resist violence through nonviolent means and to resolve conflicts using peaceful methods."[2] In the Indian context the practice of nonviolent resistance is called *satyagraha*. Practice of it can take several forms, including noncooperation, protests, boycotts, and strikes.

1. Quoted in Jessie Carney Smith and Linda T. Wynn, eds. *Freedom Facts and Firsts: 400 Years of the African American Civil Rights Experience.* Detroit: Visible Ink, 2009, p. 50.
2. Anthony Parel. "Nonviolence." In *New Dictionary of the History of Ideas*, edited by Maryanne Cline Horowitz. Farmington Hills, MI: Thomson Gale, 2005.

The primary tactic of nonviolent protest used by civil rights advocates was inspired by Indian Mohandas Ghandi. Gandhi led a nonviolent movement that ended Great Britain's rule of India in the 1930s.

little violence resulted. After relatively few problems in Virginia, Kentucky, and Tennessee, however, the travelers ran into trouble in North Carolina. Several of them, including Rustin, were arrested and sentenced to thirty days of hard labor on a chain gang for refusing to sit in the designated seating area for blacks. Shortly thereafter, the Journey of Reconciliation came to an end. Historian Lisa Cozzens elaborates: "Clearly the South, even the more moderate upper South, was not ready for integration."[12] The riders had discovered that the southern states still had laws that upheld segregation on public transit, which gave the states grounds to arrest and sentence the riders. These states were treating the Supreme Court decision as if it did not exist.

When the riders returned to Washington on April 23, there was no media coverage to mark their return. This first freedom ride had demonstrated that nonviolent direct action could be a successful tool in the civil rights fight. But the journey had not resulted in any desegregation or mass protest at the local level. While a few other black bus passengers had moved into white sections, joining the Journey of Reconciliation riders, there had been little support from the general masses in the cities they visited. The organizers of the journey were disappointed that black citizens had not joined the protest, and the civil rights activists did not expect the situation in the South to change anytime soon.

Brown v. Board of Education

Immediately following the failure of the Journey of Reconciliation to effect any change in the South, little action occurred in the fight against segregation. There were a few protests during the next few years, but little actual change in the South. The first real challenge to the Jim Crow laws came not in the field of transportation, but in public schooling.

In the field of education, black and white children attended separate schools that were unequal in every respect. Most black schools were little more than dilapidated shacks without desks or chairs. The books were hand-me-downs from white schools and were often worn-out and out-of-date. In addition, the books presented history from a white supremacist point of view; little mention was made of African Americans other than as slaves and servants.

In the early 1950s the NAACP began to look for a case that would challenge the inequality in education. They found that case in the person of Linda Brown, a seven-year-old girl in Topeka, Kansas. Despite the fact that there was a good white school only blocks from the Brown home, Linda had to walk miles to reach her bus stop to attend the black school. When the Browns tried to enroll their daughter at the nearby white school, they were turned away. The NAACP legal team decided the Browns had sufficient cause to challenge the law.

Combining Linda's case with several others, the NAACP filed an appeal with the Supreme Court: the case of *Brown v. Board of Education of Topeka, Kansas*. The legal team argued that separate facilities could never be equal. This inequality subjected blacks to such inferior conditions that it prevented a good education and was damaging to them as human beings. The arguments were based on the Fourteenth Amendment, which guarantees all citizens equal protection under the law. The NAACP's challenge was successful. On May 17, 1954, the Supreme Court ruled that separate was not equal and demanded that schools desegregate. In the unanimous decision, Chief Justice Earl Warren read:

> Today education is perhaps the most important function of state and local governments. . . . We come then to the question presented: Does segregation of children in public schools solely on the basis of race . . . deprive the children of the minority group of equal educational opportunities? We believe that it does. . . . We conclude that in the field of public education, the doctrine of "separate but equal" has no place.[13]

The Supreme Court, however, failed to outline how this inequality should be corrected. Nor did it provide a timeline for implementation of the new law. Because of these omissions by the court, segregation did not come to an end in southern schools or in any other form of southern life.

Montgomery Bus Boycott

The next significant challenge to segregation took place in Montgomery, Alabama, on December 1, 1955, when black seamstress and civil rights activist Rosa Parks refused to give up her seat for a white passenger on a city bus. Segregation laws requiring separate

In Montgomery, Alabama, African Americans walk to work during the bus boycott.

seating for blacks on public transportation were still the rule in the state of Alabama. Because she had disobeyed the law in Montgomery, Parks was arrested and fined.

Her arrest sparked a movement that spread to the entire African American community in Montgomery. Led by emerging civil rights leader Martin Luther King Jr., then a young minister in the city, the black citizens of Montgomery banded together to protest the segregation that was found on the city buses. Rather than ride the bus to work, thousands of blacks formed carpools, walked to work, or simply stayed home. On the first day of the boycott, December 5, over 90 percent of Montgomery's black citizens stayed off the buses. That figure would rise to nearly 100 percent in the year that followed.

The boycott, or avoidance of the buses, went on for more than a year. Montgomery blacks were protesting Montgomery laws that mandated segregated seating on city buses. Finally, on June 5, 1956, a federal district court ruled in *Browder v. Gayle* that segregation on public buses in Montgomery was unconstitutional. The U.S. Supreme Court later upheld the district court ruling, declaring racial segregation on all buses unconstitutional. Montgomery officials were ordered to desegregate their buses. Forty-seven other southern cities followed the Montgomery lead and also integrated their city buses. But in over half of the southern regions, the local bus lines took no action, and their facilities remained segregated. For several years following the bus boycott, there was little additional direct action or protest undertaken by civil rights organizations.

Chapter Two

Prelude and Beginnings of the Journey

Despite the victory in Montgomery and the success of desegregating a few public schools, the civil rights movement was still in its infancy. As the 1960s opened, nearly every southern city boasted some kind of local civil rights organization, but there were no plans for further direct action or other challenges to segregation.

The National Association for the Advancement of Colored People (NAACP) was still determined to fight the battle for equal rights through the courts. NAACP leaders did not want anything to do with what they considered radical techniques, such as protest marches and demonstrations. Even Martin Luther King Jr., who had spearheaded the bus boycott in Montgomery, seemed reluctant to move forward. At the same time, the Congress of Racial Equality (CORE) and the nonviolent movement also fell into a period of steady decline.

African Americans and civil rights activists faced an increasingly militant white South after the bus boycott. White southerners were opposed to desegregation and were prepared to use violence if necessary to stop it from happening.

Political Climate

Despite an upsurge in aggression from white supremacy groups and the lack of momentum from civil rights groups, the 1960s opened with a glimmer of hope and optimism for African Americans. For instance, in August 1957 the federal government had enacted the first civil rights legislation in over eighty years. It reaffirmed black voting rights under the Fifteenth Amendment and created the U.S. Commission on Civil Rights. The commission was given the responsibility of investigating and making recommendations on civil rights matters. Despite the creation of this organization, there was no movement toward ending segregation, due to resistance by white southerners who controlled Congress.

Hopes that there would be additional civil rights legislation heightened during the 1960 presidential election. Vice President Richard Nixon was running against Democratic candidate and senator John F. Kennedy of Massachusetts. Kennedy garnered thousands of votes

The 1960 presidential election between John F. Kennedy, left, and Richard Nixon, right, brought the civil rights movement into national politics. Kennedy won the black vote by promising to address racial inequality.

from blacks in the South by speaking of a need for civil rights legislation and promising to address the racial inequality in the United States. Lisa Cozzens explains: "John F. Kennedy was elected in large part due to widespread support among blacks who believed that Kennedy was more sympathetic to the civil rights movement than his opponent, Richard Nixon. Once in office, however, Kennedy proved less committed to the movement than he had appeared during the campaign."[14]

The election year also saw significant historical events occurring in Africa, which inspired civil rights activists in the United States. Freedom Rider John Lewis elaborates: "Amazing changes were happening in Africa where Ghana had won its independence a year earlier and was opening up black African liberation movements in Zaire, Somalia, Nigeria and the Congo. Here were black people thousands of miles away, achieving liberation and independence from nations that had ruled them for centuries, free."[15] Many black activists began to dream of similar changes occurring in the United States. Civil rights for blacks in the American South, however, did not appear to be imminent.

The Student Sit-In

At Woolworth and other stores in the South, blacks still had to sit outside or at separate stand-up snack bars if they wanted something to eat after shopping. In 1960 the Greensboro Four, as they were soon called, decided to change that. Four African American college freshmen, Ezell Blair Jr., David Richmond, Joseph McNeil, and Franklin McCain, tired of waiting for the federal government to act, decided to step forward in an act opposing segregation. On February 1, 1960, these students from the Agricultural and Technical College of North Carolina in Greensboro sat down at a white lunch counter in a Woolworth department store and refused to move. White customers sat down nearby and were quickly served, but no waitresses approached the blacks. Finally, one waitress told them they would have to leave and she could not serve them, stating: "I'm sorry. We don't serve coloreds in here."[16]

The following day the original four students were joined by two others; they sat at the counter for over four hours without being served. By the third day, black students occupied sixty-three of the sixty-six seats at the lunch counter. They were still refused service. When news of the demonstration at Woolworth spread, students from surrounding colleges in Greensboro, both black and white, joined the protest. By the end of the fourth day, there were demonstrations at all the segregated restaurants in the city.

The news of the "sit-ins," as they came to be called, spread throughout the South, and within a week there were sit-ins in fifteen cities in nine different southern states. Historian Herb Boyd explains the significance of the actions taken by these young people: "They gave notice that a new breed of student had emerged in the South and they were ready to confront the inequities that for too long had smothered their opportunities and stifled their dreams."[17]

The sit-ins continued for five months before Woolworth, whose stores were in virtually every major city in the United States, agreed to desegregate its lunch counters. By the end of the sit-ins eighteen months later, over seventy thousand people had taken part in the demonstrations, which occurred as far west as Nevada and as far north as Ohio. Over three thousand students were arrested and served time in jail. As a result of the sit-ins, over one hundred southern communities began desegregating their lunch counters and restaurants.

For James Farmer, the leader of CORE and an organizer of the Journey of Reconciliation, the four students symbolized a change of mood among African Americans. He later stated: "Up until then, we had accepted segregation, begrudgingly, but we had accepted it. We had spoken against it . . . but no one had defied segregation. . . . But these four freshmen sat in at the lunch counter . . . and refused to leave. This sparked a movement throughout the South."[18]

The Nashville Movement

One of the sit-in movements that had the most impact on local laws and institutions occurred in Nashville, Tennessee. Hundreds of students there took part in very visible and well-organized demonstrations at local stores in the first half of 1960. They were encouraged and, in part, led by James Lawson, an African American theology student at Vanderbilt University in Nashville, who had been conducting nonviolent workshops in the city for

On February 2, 1960, four North Carolina college students (from left) Joseph McNeil, Franklin McCain, Billy Smith, and Clarence Henderson, participate in a sit-in at a Woolworth whites-only lunch counter to address racial inequality.

several years. Lawson had taught the students not to fight back when confronted with violence. By not fighting back, the students won thousands of supporters due to their calm and peaceful behavior.

On February 27, 1960, the Nashville sit-ins were marred by violence when a group of white Nashville teenagers attacked the sit-in students. None of the students fought back. When the Nashville police arrived, they arrested eighty-one of the protesters for disorderly conduct; none of the white teens was charged. Such incidents were repeated throughout the South; some student protesters were beaten with clubs by the police, while others were subjected to tear gas; a few were attacked by police dogs. None fought back.

The Nashville sit-ins culminated in a large protest march on city hall on April 19, 1960. Two thousand students, university faculty members, and black townspeople marched together, demanding a meeting with Nashville mayor Ben West. At the time, this was the largest protest march for civil rights that had occurred in U.S. history. By the time the crowd reached the courthouse steps, the protest group had grown to five thousand individuals.

When the crowd encountered West, Diane Nash, one of the leaders of the Nashville Student Movement, asked him if he favored desegregating the lunch counters. West reluctantly said yes. Within a month, city officials and store owners agreed to integrate the stores' restaurants. Lewis elaborates: "Six downtown Nashville stores we had marched on, sat in, and been arrested at . . . served food to black customers [on May 10, 1960] for the first time in the city's history."[19]

The nonviolent action used in the sit-ins brought a new burst of energy to the movement for equality. Kneel-ins occurred at white churches, and in Biloxi, Mississippi, some young blacks there conducted a wade-in at a beach. Other young people held sit-ins in public libraries, movie theaters, courtrooms, and skating rinks.

By refusing to wait for change, students in Nashville and across the South had succeeded in desegregating hundreds of restaurants. By using only peaceful and direct action, they had drawn national attention and inspired tens of thousands of citizens to take a more active role in the civil rights movement. Historian Benjamin Quarles elaborates: "The sit-in movement stirred the conscience of the South and of the nation."[20]

On February, 27, 1960, white teenagers attacked protesters at a Nashville lunch counter sit-in. A Freedom Rider lies on the floor, holding his head after being dragged off his stool and beaten.

The Student Nonviolent Coordinating Committee

During the sit-ins in Nashville and other southern cities, the Southern Christian Leadership Conference (SCLC), a civil rights organization founded in 1957 and led by King, decided to sponsor a youth leaders' conference to discuss future student participation in the larger civil rights movement. Hundreds of students from all over the United States attended this conference, held at Shaw University in Raleigh, North Carolina.

Though the SCLC had hoped to gain control of the students' activities so it could direct their actions, the students ended up founding an independent organization called the Student Nonviolent Coordinating Committee (SNCC) on April 17, 1960. The SNCC became the first organization created by and for the younger generation of civil rights activists. The SNCC also became the first group to use the terms *nonviolent* and *nonviolence* in its name and charter: "We affirm the philosophical or religious ideal of nonviolence as the foundation of our purpose, the presupposition of our faith, and the manner of our action. . . . By appealing to the conscience and standing on the moral nature of human existence, nonviolence nurtures the atmosphere in which reconciliation and justice become actual possibilities."[21] The organization, however, also stated firmly that nonviolence did not mean nonaction.

The members of the SNCC immediately called for direct action against segregation, suggesting that the existing civil rights organizations were being too cautious. Historian David Halberstam, who in 1960 was a young reporter writing for the local newspaper the *Tennessean* in Nashville, explains: "To the students, the NAACP was old hat . . . [it] had become the voice of the black bourgeoisie. Its strategy depended too much on the courts. The great resource which the NAACP was neglecting was the growing power of black people to act on their own."[22]

The young activists also demanded an end to Jim Crow laws and planned to use nonviolent demonstrations and protests to end discrimination in the South. In an SNCC newsletter published in June 1960, the organization stated: "We want the world to know that we no longer accept the inferior position of second-class citizenship. We are going to go to jail, be ridiculed, spat upon, and even suffer physical violence to obtain First Class Citizenship."[23]

James Lawson

Born in Pennsylvania, James Lawson, an African American, went to Baldwin-Wallace College, Boston University, and Oberlin University. Lawson was a conscientious objector, and during the Korean War he chose to go to jail rather than fight. Afterward, he went to India for three years as a foreign missionary, where he studied Mohandas Gandhi's teachings on nonviolence.

In 1960 Lawson was a divinity student at Vanderbilt University in Nashville, Tennessee. While nonviolence had already been used by Martin Luther King Jr. during the Birmingham bus boycott, it was Lawson who helped hundreds of young Nashville students learn this principle. He held workshops in Nashville for over a year and prepared these students, black and white, for the student sit-ins, Freedom Rides, and other challenges that lay ahead during the civil rights struggle.

Lawson taught the young blacks to take pride in themselves and understand that fighting for equality was a noble cause. His primary goal was to teach the students not to be ashamed of their black heritage. Many black Americans felt shame because of their second-class citizenship. Lawson helped change this mindset by constantly affirming their worth and emphasizing Christian doctrines about God's love.

Lawson later participated in the Freedom Rides and was eventually expelled from Vanderbilt University for his roles in the student sit-ins and the Freedom Rides.

On May 1, 1960, James Lawson Jr., far left, leads a discussion on sit-in protests. The tactics worked. Ten days later, six Nashville restaurants that had experienced sit-ins served black customers for the first time.

Boynton v. Virginia

As a result of the successful student sit-ins, momentum began to increase among young civil rights activists throughout the South, and the students and civil rights organizations began to look for another way to challenge segregation. The specific direction of this challenge came from another Supreme Court decision.

In 1958 Bruce Boynton, a black student at Howard University Law School in Washington, D.C., boarded a Trailways bus bound for his home in Montgomery, Alabama. During a stopover in Richmond, Virginia, Boynton went in the bus terminal restaurant to get something to eat. He sat down at a stool in the whites-only section, where he was refused service and ordered to move to the black section. When he refused to do so, the manager called the police, who arrested the young man for trespassing. Boynton was convicted of disobeying Virginia segregation laws.

Boynton, stating that he was protected by federal desegregation laws stemming from the *Morgan v. Virginia* ruling of 1946,

Freedom Songs

Toward the end of the Nashville sit-ins, the students led a group of five thousand demonstrators in a spontaneous march on city hall to plead with the mayor to end segregation at the city's lunch counters. As the crowd gathered on the steps of the courthouse, Guy Carawan, one of the young demonstrators, began playing his guitar and singing. The song he chose was an old black spiritual called "I'll Overcome Someday." The words, however, had been changed: "We shall overcome some day . . . Oh deep in my heart, I do believe, that we shall overcome some day."

The song electrified the crowd, which was soon joining in the singing. It was easy to sing and expressed many of the long-held grievances of African Americans, along with the hope that someday things would change for the better. The song, retitled "We Shall Overcome" and sung by folksinger and activist Pete Seeger, became the anthem of the civil rights movement.

Quoted in Kansas State University American Studies."We Shall Overcome." www.k-state.edu/english/nelp/american.studies.s98/we.shall.overcome.html.

decided to appeal his conviction. He claimed: "Arresting a black interstate bus passenger for refusing to leave a whites-only section of a bus station restaurant violated . . . the Equal Protection Clause of the United States Constitution."[24]

Boynton found support from the NAACP and its legal team. After hearing arguments from both sides, the U.S. Supreme Court made its ruling on December 5, 1960. The court ruled in favor of Boynton, stating that restaurant facilities in interstate bus terminals could not discriminate on the basis of race. The court ruled in a 7–2 decision that "bus transportation was related to interstate commerce, and that racial segregation in public transportation, including terminals, was illegal."[25]

As with past Supreme Court rulings on segregation, enforcing this new law proved to be a challenge. In fact, the majority of whites in the South simply ignored the federal ruling and continued to segregate public facilities and interstate travel.

James Farmer and the Freedom Ride

After the Supreme Court's ruling, CORE decided to challenge the South's nonobservance of the federal law requiring integration in interstate transportation. Two members of CORE, Tom Gaither and Gordon Carey, had discussed the idea of a freedom ride on a long bus trip from South Carolina to New York. Sitting in the segregated bus, the idea to test the new court decision seemed appropriate and exciting. After Gaither and Carey presented their idea to CORE, the leader of that organization, Farmer, immediately determined that these two men had the right idea.

As the idea of a freedom ride grew in Farmer's mind, he asked Gaither to make a scouting trip to the South. Gaither surveyed the layouts of various bus terminals and facilities and met with black leaders along the way. He made arrangements with these leaders for housing and speaking engagements for the riders. Gaither also observed the local racial relations in a variety of towns and cities. In nearly every community he visited, Gaither found some support for the ride and was able to find sponsors in dozens of places. Though heartened by his reception in the upper South, Gaither was shocked by the defiance he found in Alabama and Mississippi. He identified a number of cities where the riders would probably encounter violence.

As James L. Farmer and CORE put together plans for the Freedom Rides, they identified a number of southern cities where the riders would likely encounter resistance—such as this "Out-of-Order" sign—and violence.

Despite the potential for violence, Farmer wanted to proceed with the Freedom Ride. He saw the ride as a natural progression of the sit-in movement. Because of the outpouring of support from students all over the South during the lunch counter demonstrations, Farmer hoped the ride would produce a similar response. He hoped to stir things up to the point where average black citizens would begin to demand changes.

Farmer also readily admitted that another purpose of the rides was to deliberately violate the Jim Crow laws of the South in order to get southern racists to create a crisis of violence. Only then, Farmer believed, would the federal government enforce the court's decision. Farmer explained: "Why didn't the federal government enforce its law? We decided it was because of politics. If we were right in assuming that the federal government did not enforce federal law because of its fear of reprisals from the South, then what we had to do was to make it more dangerous politically for the federal government not to enforce federal law."[26] Farmer hoped that the ride would compel other civil rights organizations to pressure the government for enforcement. In addition, he hoped that any violence would garner national news headlines and embarrass the government into taking action.

Preparations for the Ride

Once the decision was made to set the Freedom Ride in motion, notices were sent out to civil rights organizations and colleges throughout the United States. James Peck, a white veteran of the 1947 Journey of Reconciliation, was one of the first to volunteer for the Freedom Ride. Lewis, one of the leaders of the Nashville Student Movement, was also quick to offer his services. Lewis explains: "I immediately wrote for an application. When it arrived, it contained detailed warnings about violence and arrests. . . . I wasn't frightened. On the contrary, I was elated. And eager."[27] In all, there were thirteen riders accepted for the first Freedom Ride. The group was a mixture of black and white, male and female, old and young, religious and secular.

The volunteers were told that one group would travel on a Greyhound bus; the other on a Continental Trailways bus. They would leave Washington, D.C., on May 4, 1961. They hoped to arrive in New Orleans, the final destination, by May 17, the seventh anniversary of the *Brown v. Board of Education* decision. The ride, thirteen days long, would traverse Virginia, the Carolinas, Georgia, Alabama, and Mississippi.

When the riders arrived in Washington, D.C., the departure point, they underwent training that included intense role-playing sessions. During these, some members of the group played riders, while others played white segregationists. Rider Benjamin Cox recalls that various individuals were knocked down, spit upon, and shoved around. In addition, racial epithets were used, all in preparation for the harassment that was sure to occur during the Freedom Ride.

The riders were also given training in nonviolence and legal information. They were told, for instance, that they were breaking no laws, that the Supreme Court in the *Boynton v. Virginia* case had forbidden segregation in interstate transportation. Farmer stressed: "This was not civil disobedience really, because we [were] . . . doing what the Supreme Court said we had a right to do."[28] The riders were merely asking that the law be enforced.

Farmer also issued strict instructions on how the riders were to dress: suits and ties for the men, dresses and heels for the women. The riders were also given instructions on seating arrangements. The Reverend B. Elton Cox, one of the original riders and a minister in High Point, North Carolina, describes the seating arrangements: "The blacks would ride up front and the whites would ride in the rear, which gave the other passengers a shock because that wasn't the arrangement they were expecting. And when we got to each stop, the blacks would go into the white waiting room and drink out of the white fountains and go into the white rest rooms, and the whites would go in the old colored; and that shocked everybody."[29] In addition, one interracial pair was designated to sit in adjoining seats on each bus. This was done to challenge the segregation law that stated that blacks were forbidden to sit next to whites.

As the training was finishing up, Farmer wrote a personal letter to President Kennedy informing him of the ride and requesting that the law be enforced. Letters were also sent to the Federal Bureau of Investigation (FBI), the Justice Department, and the two bus companies. Farmer did not receive a reply from any of these sources.

The Reverend Martin Luther King Jr., third from right, at a Freedom Ride planning meeting. Organizers held training sessions that included role-playing sessions on how to deal with anticipated violence against the riders.

Virginia to Georgia

As the buses entered the South on May 4, 1961, signs of discrimination and prejudice were everywhere. One of the Freedom Riders, William Mahoney, commented: "At our first stop in Virginia . . . I was confronted with what the Southern white has called 'separate but equal.' A modern rest station with gleaming counters and picture windows was labeled 'White,' and a small wooden shack beside it was tagged 'Colored.'"[30]

In Petersburg, Virginia, the riders were received warmly and were encouraged by the support of fifty-five sit-in veterans. The riders spoke to black college students and black church congregations

The Jail-No-Bail Initiative

During the formation of the Student Nonviolent Coordinating Committee, a workshop recommended that all future demonstrators choose jail over bail. A person who is arrested can deposit a determined amount of money, called bail, with the court and be released until it is time to appear in court. Then, if the arrested person does not return to face the charges, the court can keep the money. Where serious crimes have been committed, deputies or bounty hunters are usually sent to physically retrieve the person.

The tactic of choosing jail over bail was most effective during the Freedom Rides. Officials in Jackson, Mississippi, in particular, were hoping the riders would post bail and then leave without trial, sparing that city the expense of holding a trial. When the demonstrators refused to post such bail, the system was thrown into confusion. Ernest "Rip" Patton, one of the Freedom Riders, elaborates: "The fine might be a $50 fine and the sentence might be 31 days, but we would choose the 31 days. It makes it hard on the system to have to feed and take care of a lot of students that they really didn't expect to do that with."[1]

Diane Nash, one of the leaders of the Nashville Student Movement, explained the reasoning behind the initiative: "We feel that if we pay these fines, we would be contributing to and supporting the injustice and immoral practices that have been performed in the arrest and conviction of the defendants."[2]

1. Quoted in *Talk of the Nation*. "Remembering the Freedom Rides, 50 Years Later." National Public Radio, May 5, 2011. www.npr.org/2011/05/05/136025553/freedom-riders-risked-their-lives-for-equality.
2. Quoted in Herb Boyd. *We Shall Overcome*. Naperville, IL: Sourcebooks, 2004, p. 93.

along the way. In Salisbury, North Carolina, two black women, regular passengers on the bus, had the courage to follow the example of the riders and demand service at a white lunch counter in the bus terminal. All were served in a courteous manner.

The first real trouble came in Rock Hill, South Carolina, when John Lewis became the first rider to be assaulted. The group was surrounded by a group of young white men, one of whom punched Lewis in the face. Despite the violence, Lewis and the others were determined to proceed. Shortly after this incident,

Lewis, planning a career as a missionary, was called away from the ride to interview for a position overseas, but he planned to rejoin the riders in Birmingham, Alabama.

From South Carolina, the buses proceeded into Georgia. Here the ride was violence free; the political leaders in that state had chosen not to defy the Supreme Court ruling by harassing or arresting the riders. The riders got through Georgia without incident and, in fact, held a big, well-attended rally in Atlanta. There the riders met King, who praised their efforts. He shook each rider's hand but then warned them that they would not make it through Alabama without trouble.

Despite the level of training the riders received, none of them was prepared for what lay ahead. Sunday, May 14, 1961, was Mother's Day. Farmer left the ride that morning because his father was near death. The other riders left Atlanta in two buses headed for Birmingham, Alabama. Only one bus would make it there.

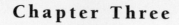

Chapter Three

The Ride
Gets Bumpy

Despite warnings of violence from Martin Luther King Jr. and other civil rights activists, the riders proceeded into the state of Alabama, heading for Birmingham. None of them anticipated the violent reception they would receive.

While racial violence was present in the entire South, it was more deeply entrenched and visible in the Deep South states of Alabama and Mississippi. Historian David Halberstam explains what the riders were up against: "The forces of segregation, already angered by various developments in the past seven years, the increasing access of the integrationists to the national media, and what seemed to them the mounting arrogance of the black leadership, particularly Martin Luther King, Jr. were already on a hair trigger, most itching for a fight, particularly . . . on their own sacred terrain."[31] Many segregationists were secretly delighted that the Freedom Riders were coming, because of the opportunity for confrontation.

The Ku Klux Klan, a violent racist group, was very powerful in Alabama. Its members believed that the white race was superior, and they were willing to resort to the worst kind of violence, such as lynching, to keep racial inequality intact. The Klan had come into existence in the South after the Civil War and had been

The Ku Klux Klan held rallies across Mississippi and Alabama to make plans for confronting the Freedom Riders with violence.

very active in violent attacks against blacks who tried to succeed and advance in society. Klansmen, dressed in white hoods and robes to hide their features, spread death and terror throughout black communities, often burning crosses in the yards of those blacks—and whites—who did not accept segregation.

In Alabama the Klan had known about the ride since the middle of April because of a series of FBI memos sent to the Birmingham police. The Klan was aided by white supremacist local leaders and members of the police department in several Alabama towns. The group's plan was to begin with an assault on one of the buses outside Anniston, Alabama. This would be followed by more violence in Birmingham, where the Klan hoped to stop the Freedom Ride once and for all.

The Bus Bombing

Unaware of the Klan's plan, the seven Freedom Riders on the first bus entered the state of Alabama. Also on board this bus were two undercover agents from the Alabama Highway Patrol. One of these men was E.L. Cowling, sent by Alabama director of public safety Floyd Mann to prevent anyone from being killed. The bus, a Greyhound, headed toward Anniston, a town known for its racist practices.

As the riders pulled into Anniston, a crowd of nearly two hundred Klansmen was waiting for them. The Klan, having been given permission by local law enforcement officials to strike against the riders without fear of arrest, was ready for action. Seeing the mob gathered, the driver of the bus yelled: "Well, boys, here they are. I brought you some n——s and n——lovers."[32]

The mob, brandishing baseball bats and clubs, immediately rushed toward the bus, slashing its tires. Edward Blankenheim, a student at the University of Arizona, describes the riders' reception in Anniston: "We drove into Anniston to the bus station, and the mob surrounded the bus . . . they were ugly, ugly people. . . . They wanted us dead."[33]

The riders decided not to disembark, and the Greyhound bus limped out of the depot on its slashed tires, followed by fifty cars filled with over two hundred angry whites. The bus's tires went flat about 5 miles (8km) outside Anniston, and the driver fled the bus. The mob moved in, using bricks and a heavy ax to smash all the windows in the bus.

A firebomb was then thrown into the bus. Thick, black smoke filled the bus's interior, making it difficult for the riders to breathe. While the riders were struggling for air, the white mob surrounded the bus, yelling obscenities and racial epithets. Civil rights activist John Lewis later wrote about the Anniston incident: "Even now . . . the picture is stunning to look at. It's like a scene out of Bosnia. . . . Those were American men who had clutched pipes and clubs and bricks. . . . Those were Americans shouting and cursing and beating on the windows."[34]

Just when it looked like the riders might die from the flames and smoke, the bus's gas tank exploded. When the mob pulled back from the flames, the riders escaped. Hank Thomas was one of the first to leave the bus. He was met by a man who asked if he was okay. As Thomas nodded his head, he was hit with a baseball bat. "The next thing I knew," Thomas states, "I was on the ground."[35] A number of the other riders were also beaten to the ground, where they lay bloodied and helpless. Many of the riders were saved from further violence by Cowling, who, gun in hand, drove the mob off to prevent them from lynching the riders.

As the violence subsided, Freedom Riders and other passengers lay on the ground, gasping for breath and crying for help.

Janie Forsyth McKinney, a twelve-year-old white girl who lived nearby, came to the riders' assistance, providing them with water. Fifty years later she described what she witnessed: "It was horrible. It was like a scene from hell. It was the worst suffering I'd ever heard."[36] For daring to help the injured riders, she and her family were later ostracized and forced to leave the county.

The riders were eventually taken to safety by local civil rights activist Reverend Fred Shuttlesworth, who arrived with a caravan of church deacons. Eight cars, loaded with black men carrying shotguns and rifles, drove the riders to Birmingham to wait for the second bus.

The bombing of the bus made national news headlines and led network television news. Historian Taylor Branch elaborates: "A photographer took a shot of the flames leaping out the front window of the abandoned bus, with a thick column of smoke rising from windows all along the sides. By the evening, this photograph

Five miles outside of Anniston, Alabama, a Freedom Ride bus was firebombed by a white mob armed with pipes and baseball bats.

Fred Shuttlesworth

Born in 1922 in Mulgar, Alabama, Fred Lee Shuttlesworth grew up in the Jim Crow South. In 1956, when the state of Alabama made it illegal to be a member of the National Association for the Advancement of Colored People (NAACP), Shuttlesworth founded the Alabama Christian Movement for Human Rights. He was also a cofounder of the Southern Christian Leadership Conference (SCLC) and served as the organization's first secretary. He supported the Montgomery bus boycott in 1955 and was active in voter registration in Birmingham. He has been described by many, including Martin Luther King Jr., as one of the most courageous civil rights fighters in the South.

During the Freedom Rides, Shuttlesworth protected many of the riders in his own home, arranged a system with Diane Nash to convey riders from Tennessee to Alabama, and spoke out frequently in support of the riders. Journalist Andrew M. Manis states: "Fred Shuttlesworth is clearly one of the most unsung of the many heroes of the American Civil Rights movement. . . . No one in the civil rights movement more resolutely and directly confronted segregation than Shuttlesworth." The Freedom Riders agreed that they would never have gotten out of Alabama alive without Shuttlesworth.

He moved to Cincinnati in late 1961 and became the pastor at Revelation Baptist Church. He later organized the Greater Light Baptist Church and was instrumental in helping to elect the first black mayor in Cincinnati history. He also continued his civil rights work on a national level and was instru-

mental in establishing the Birmingham Civil Rights Institute. A statue of Shuttlesworth now greets visitors to that location. He retired from the pulpit in 2006 at age eighty-four and returned to Birmingham the following year. Shuttlesworth died in October 2011. The Birmingham airport now bears his name.

Andrew M. Manis. "Birmingham's Reverend Fred Shuttlesworth: Unsung Hero of the Civil Rights Movement." *Baptist History and Heritage*, June 22, 2000.

When Alabama outlawed the NAACP, Fred Shuttlesworth founded the Alabama Christian Movement for Human Rights in response.

would move on both the national and international wires for distribution around the world."[37]

The Klan Waits in Birmingham

Meanwhile, the second bus, a Trailways, had also entered the state of Alabama. There were a number of Ku Klux Klansmen on board. Even before the bus arrived at its destination, violence broke out. Two white riders, James Peck and Walter Bergman, a sixty-two-year-old retired professor from Michigan, were beaten severely. Peck was pulled from his seat and beaten until his face was bloody. Bergman was beaten to his knees and kicked repeatedly in the rib cage. Herb Boyd explains that Bergman was, in fact, "attacked so savagely that he sustained permanent brain damage and had a stroke that would leave him paralyzed for the rest of his life."[38]

The bus driver ignored what was happening and continued toward Birmingham. According to historians, Birmingham at that time was considered "perhaps the most segregated city in the nation."[39] The city was often referred to as "Bombingham" because of all the bombs the Klan had used to destroy black churches and homes.

The Klan also had the support of one of the city's most powerful officials, Commissioner of Public Safety Eugene "Bull" Connor. Civil rights activist Julian Bond offered his opinion about Connor: "[Birmingham was] literally a police state. . . . [Connor was] just rabid on the issue of race. Birmingham was his city and he was determined to make sure the Freedom Riders knew that."[40]

Prior to the bus's arrival in Birmingham, police sergeant Tom Cook, an active member of the Klan and under orders from Connor, told Klan leaders: "We're going to allow you fifteen minutes. . . . You can beat 'em, bomb 'em, maim 'em, kill 'em. . . . There will be absolutely no arrests."[41] Connor later explained why he had ordered the police off the scene: "It was time to let . . . the Kennedys, the Communists, and all the other meddling South-haters know that the loyal sons of Alabama were ready to fight and die for white supremacy and states' rights. It was time for the blood to flow."[42]

Mother's Day at the Depot

With the support of the local police, a large white mob surrounded the second bus when it arrived in Birmingham. The riders were dragged to the pavement and beaten with clubs and lead pipes. With their pledge of nonviolence, the riders were defenseless and woefully outnumbered. Peck, with blood dripping down his face, later needed fifty stitches in his head to close the wound.

Howard K. Smith of CBS News was on the scene and described what he had seen: "When the bus arrived, the toughs grabbed the passengers into alleys and corridors, pounding them with pipes, key rings, and with fists. One passenger was knocked down at my feet by twelve of the hoodlums and his face was beaten and kicked until it was a bloody pulp."[43] That night Americans, while watching television, saw white men with clubs and the bloody faces of Freedom Riders who had refused to return the violence.

Later a reporter asked Connor why the police had not intervened. Connor explained: "We try to let off as many of our policemen as possible so they can spend Mother's Day at home with their families."[44] The following day Alabama representative George Huddleston, in a speech to Congress, defended the police: "It is difficult for any Southerner who understands the problem confronting the people to sympathize with this radical extremist group which has invaded our state. They got just what they asked for."[45]

The Federal Government's Response

When news of the Alabama violence reached the White House, John F. Kennedy and his brother, Attorney General Robert Kennedy, were both sickened by what had happened. Despite visual evidence of wrongdoing by the Klan, however, the brothers tended to blame the riders for what had happened. As far as President Kennedy was concerned, the rides were causing him political problems and embarrassing him both in the United States and overseas.

President Kennedy felt uneasy about civil rights issues, and although he sympathized with the plight of blacks in the South, he did not want to involve the federal government. Kennedy, however, knew that the racial hatred demonstrated in Alabama was a serious blow to America's image abroad. Halberstam explains the Kennedys' position: "The Kennedys . . . while paying lip service to supporting civil rights, were most decidedly unenthusiastic about the Freedom Rides. They did not want a bunch of integrationists going through the Deep South, causing . . . political trouble,

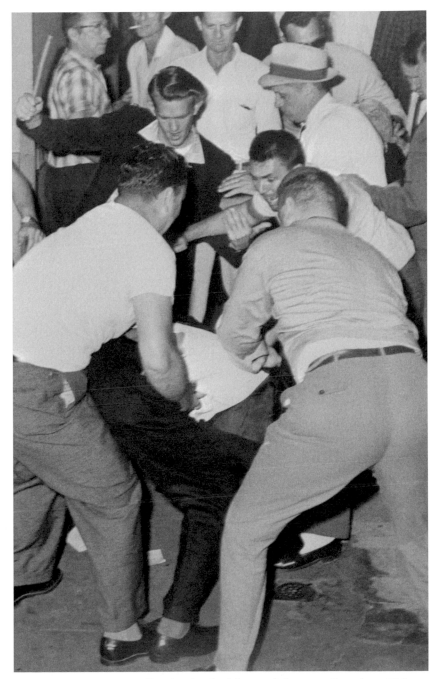

On May 14, 1961, a police-backed white mob beats a Freedom Rider nearly to death at the Birmingham bus depot. That night Americans saw on television the bloodied faces of riders who had refused to resort to violence to protect themselves.

Bull Connor

Theophilus Eugene "Bull" Connor was born in 1897 and grew up in Alabama. In 1921 he was asked to fill in for a sick baseball announcer in Dallas, Texas. As a baseball commentator, Connor earned the nickname "Bull" because of his booming voice.

Despite having never completed high school, Connor served in the Alabama House of Representatives for several years and then was appointed Birmingham's commissioner of public safety from 1958 to 1963. He played a leading role in the Birmingham response to the Freedom Rides by allowing the Klan to have unimpeded access to the riders. Throughout his career, Connor was an ardent and very outspoken racist. Historian David Halberstam elaborates:

> He had quite deliberately made himself the symbol of a certain kind of white-black relationship, one in which the raw police power of white people was used as nakedly as need be to keep black people in their place. In Birmingham, he was the law. What pleased him on a given day was legal; what displeased him the next day was illegal. His fondness for pure physical force appealed to white people in Birmingham. . . . In racial matters, he was not merely the top cop, he was judge and jury as well.

Connor was eventually ousted from power. Birmingham businesspeople and city officials became convinced that Connor was a throwback to times

that had passed and was a symbol of hard-line southern racism. In 1963 Connor was replaced. Three years later, Connor suffered a stroke that left him confined to a wheelchair; he died in 1973.

David Halberstam. *The Children*. New York: Fawcett, 1998, p. 291.

Bull Connor, a die-hard racist, was Birmingham's commissioner of public safety when the Freedom Riders came to town. He allowed the Ku Klux Klan to harass and intimidate the riders.

and forcing John Kennedy to choose between his more liberal and humane impulses and the hard reality of a Democratic party still dependent on the all-white political machinery in the South."[46] The riders were trying to force him to act.

Despite the reluctance of the Kennedys to become involved, the federal government was being slowly pulled into the crisis. To compensate for a lack of more direct action, Robert Kennedy dispatched one of his associates, John Seigenthaler, to Birmingham to see what could be done about getting the riders to safety.

The FBI was also reluctant to get involved in the violent situation in the South. The FBI's director, J. Edgar Hoover, was not sympathetic to the civil rights cause and has often been identified by historians as a racist. He made no excuse for his stance against blacks and tended to see such protests as Communist inspired.

Criticism of the Freedom Rides

Hoover was not the only American who claimed the riders had Communist leanings. Senator James O. Eastland of Mississippi, in a speech to the U.S. Senate in late May 1961, stated: "The agent provocateurs who have descended upon the Southern states, in the name of 'peace riders' were sent for the sole purpose of stirring up discord, strife, and violence. 'Peace riders' is a revered Communist term."[47]

While other Americans did not use the word *Communist*, many people did criticize the riders for their radical political leanings. Many Americans were afraid that the rides would create widespread social disorder and riots in the country. White citizens of the southern states called the riders criminals, while many southern newspapers portrayed them as habitual lawbreakers. The press in many other communities also bitterly condemned what the riders were doing. While the riders would later be called heroes, in 1961 they were more often called dangerous troublemakers and radicals. The Freedom Rides were sending shock waves through American society.

Criticism also came from newspapers across the country. Editorial after editorial condemned the riders, blaming them for the violence. Scott Sines, a reporter in Spokane, Washington, disagreed with these editorials: "Some things are simply wrong. Suggesting that a movement centered on human rights was a communist plot

The Importance of the Media

Photographs and news coverage of the Anniston bus bombing and the violence in Birmingham and Montgomery were front-page stories in the nation's major newspapers. The pictures were also widely broadcast on network television. Television, in part, brought the violence and inequity in the South into the living rooms of Americans. CBS news anchor Howard K. Smith, in particular, shocked American viewers with his eyewitness accounts and pictures. The image of the burning bus in Anniston along with the bloody bodies in Birmingham were by far the most startling images yet produced from the civil rights movement.

As a result, and from that point forward, the media began to play a significant role in the civil rights movement. After news stories and photographs spread across the country, for instance, hundreds of people, young and old, came forward to risk their lives for civil rights.

Media coverage also had an impact on the federal government. The Kennedy administration was very sensitive to public opinion. The president and his advisers had seen the pictures and heard the firsthand accounts coming out of the South. With the media covering the violence, the Kennedys were very concerned that millions of Americans were viewing the images of black people being beaten while white police officers stood idly by. Soon the media was making it increasingly difficult for the president and the attorney general to stay out of the Freedom Ride crisis.

is one of them. Blaming the victims for the racially motivated attacks because they exercised their constitutional rights is another."[48]

The Riders Decide to Stop

The Freedom Riders were unaware of the arguments being made for and against them. Many of them had been treated for their injuries and found refuge in the homes of local black activists. Once rested, they went to the depot in Birmingham to wait for a bus to take them to Montgomery. At the bus station, they found both police officers and members of the Klan waiting for them.

When the bus driver refused to proceed, the riders began to discuss the situation. Concerned about further violence, they agreed that the Freedom Ride should end. Rather than go to Montgomery and face more violence, they chose to leave right away for New Orleans by plane. When they notified the Congress of Racial Equality (CORE) officials of their decision, they were told that the organization fully supported the riders' decision to terminate the Freedom Ride. Historian Todd Moye explains CORE's reasoning: "When the first wave of Freedom Riders met with a wall of vitriol and shockingly animalistic violence in Alabama, CORE faced an impossible choice: continue the rides and risk martyring the riders or acknowledge the monumentality of prosegregationist

U.S. attorney general Robert Kennedy sent Justice Department official John Seigenthaler, pictured, to Alabama to assist the Freedom Riders in getting to New Orleans.

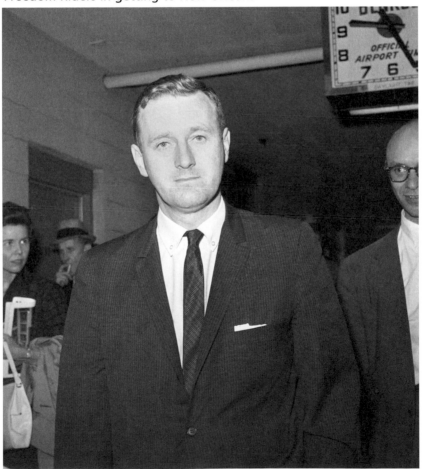

hostility and retreat from Birmingham. CORE chose the latter course and declared victory."[49]

After notifying CORE, the riders proceeded to the airport, where they discovered the Klan had once again arrived before them. Despite some harassment at the airport, the riders eventually boarded the plane, only to be sent back to the airport depot after a bomb threat was made. By this time Robert Kennedy had received word that the riders were having problems getting out of the city. When Seigenthaler, Kennedy's representative, arrived to help, he found the riders still trapped at the airport depot, surrounded by the Klan. Seigenthaler contacted Alabama officials and finally made arrangements for the riders to depart on the next flight to New Orleans. He then accompanied the riders to their destination. It appeared that the Freedom Ride was over.

In Washington, D.C., the Kennedy brothers breathed a sigh of relief. With the riders flying to New Orleans, they could focus all their energies on foreign affairs. And in Alabama, white supremacists rejoiced; their tactics had worked, and they had stopped the Freedom Rides.

But the ride would not die. In Nashville a group of students who had participated in the sit-ins were meeting and talking about resuming the Freedom Rides. The students agreed that they would not allow violence to deter them from continuing the attack on interstate segregation.

Chapter Four

The Ride Continues: Montgomery, Alabama

Diane Nash, the leader of the Nashville, Tennesee contingent of the Student Nonviolent Coordinating Committee (SNCC), was concerned when she learned that the Freedom Ride had stopped. The Nashville activists believed that ending the ride was sending the wrong message to both the federal government and the South. Nash stated: "I strongly felt that the future of the [civil rights] movement was going to be cut short if the Freedom Ride had been stopped as a result of violence."[50] She added: "The impression would have been that whenever a movement starts, all [you have to do] is attack it with massive violence and the blacks [will] stop."[51]

Nash and the others began discussing whether they should become actively involved. One of the students asked why they should be the ones to continue the Freedom Ride. John Lewis, who had been on the first part of the ride, answered: "If not us, then who? If not now, then when? Will there be a better day for it tomorrow or next year? Will it be less dangerous then? Will someone else's children have to risk their lives instead of us risking ours?"[52]

After long hours of talking, on May 16, 1961, the Nashville contingent decided to continue the Freedom Ride. Jim Zwerg, one of the white volunteers, believed that they were the logical choice to take over the Freedom Ride. "We, the Nashville students had been through the violence [of the sit-ins], had been arrested. We'd all had our lives threatened. We were the ones who had not been broken. We were the logical ones to continue."[53]

The Ride Moves Forward

Once the decision had been made, Nash contacted the Congress of Racial Equality (CORE) director James Farmer and informed him the students would continue the ride. In assuming leadership of the Freedom Ride, the SNCC and the young students in Nashville moved to the forefront in the civil rights movement. Todd Moye elaborates: "In [continuing the ride], the Nashville students . . . exposed a generational crack in the movement that would widen over the next few years. In taking the baton from CORE in this instance . . . the students assumed effective control of the movement's agenda."[54]

When Nash called Justice Department officials to tell them that the ride was going to continue, she was warned about the potential for violence. The Justice Department was not pleased, and John Seigenthaler was assigned to keep an eye on things for Robert Kennedy. Seigenthaler, in fact, told Nash: "You're going to get your people killed."[55] Nash replied: "Then others will follow them."[56]

A contingent of ten students quickly left Nashville for Birmingham, Alabama. They were determined to proceed to Montgomery, Alabama, despite more threats of violence. This group included Lewis, one of the original riders. Nash was left in charge of finding other students to join the riders.

A Midnight Ride

When the new riders arrived in Birmingham on May 17, they were immediately arrested and taken to jail. The commissioner of public safety, Bull Connor, emphasized that these arrests were for the riders' own protection. The riders spent that evening and the next day in their cells. On the second evening, Connor showed up at 11:30 P.M. and told the riders that he was taking them all

John Lewis

John Robert Lewis was twenty-one in 1961 when he joined the Freedom Ride. He was already a successful civil rights activist, having participated in the Nashville sit-ins. Lewis had grown up in Alabama and encountered racism at an early age. He made his first protest against segregation at age sixteen when he requested a library card at the all-white public library. He was refused, but he followed up by writing letters of complaint to library officials.

Lewis was one of the first volunteers to sign up for the 1961 Freedom Rides and played a leading role in the resumption of the ride following the violence in Birmingham. Following the end of the Freedom Rides, he participated and played a significant role in many key events of the civil rights era. In 1967 he graduated from Fisk University with a degree in religion and philosophy. He served as chair of the SNCC for three years. In 1968 he played a key role in former attorney general Robert Kennedy's presidential bid. In 1986 he was elected to the U.S. Congress as a representative of Georgia and is still serving in that capacity.

Lewis received the first Profiles in Courage Lifetime Achievement Award on May 21, 2001. At that time Senator Edward Kennedy, brother of President John F. Kennedy and Attorney General Robert Kennedy, stated: "Despite more than forty arrests and countless beatings, John Lewis never stopped believing in the ideals of the Constitution and the Declaration of Independence."

Quoted in Robin Washington. "JFK Award Honors Freedom Rider." *Boston Herald*, May 22, 2001.

Original Freedom Rider John R. Lewis—seen here being arrested during a protest—played a pivotal role in the resumption of the Freedom Rides. Today Lewis is a U.S. congressman from Georgia.

back to Tennessee. The prisoners were loaded into several police cars, including one driven by Connor himself. The police commissioner stopped the caravan near the tiny border town of Ardmore. The riders' luggage was placed on the side of the road, and they were told that there was a train station up the road.

One hundred miles (161km) from Nashville, the riders knew they were in a dangerous situation; they were stranded in Klan country. No media had seen them leave Birmingham, so no one other than Connor and the other police officers who drove knew where they were. They found no train station but were able to call Nashville for help. Then they found shelter with an isolated farm family living in a dilapidated shack. When they knocked on the door, a black man opened it. Lewis stated: "We're the Freedom Riders. Please let us in."[57] Initially fearful of reprisals if they took in the riders, the man said no but changed his mind at his wife's urging.

After spending the night with the family, the riders piled into the car of a Nashville man who had been sent to get them and

Fred Shuttlesworth, standing, not only protected the Freedom Riders with armed men, he also sheltered and fed them in his own home.

headed back to Birmingham. They were driven to the house of civil rights activist Fred Shuttlesworth. Additional riders from Nashville were there waiting for them. The riders ate and prayed together and then headed downtown to the bus station.

While they waited for a bus to Montgomery, Birmingham officials made it difficult for the riders by cutting the public telephone lines and closing all the snack stands. The riders, not to be deterred, began singing their freedom songs.

The Klan was also there, deliberately stepping on riders' toes, cursing the riders, blocking access to restrooms, and pouring drinks on them. The police did nothing. Finally, a driver was found, but he refused to drive the riders, stating: "I've only got one life to live, and I'm damned well not going to give it to the NAACP [National Association for the Advancement of Colored People], and I'm damn well not going to give it to CORE."[58] The riders waited all night for another driver to be found.

Finally, the original driver agreed to take the bus and the riders to Montgomery, Alabama. This was thanks, in part, to Robert Kennedy, who had pressured Alabama governor John Patterson. Catherine Burks-Brooks, one of the young Nashville students who arrived in Birmingham to continue the ride, describes the situation: "It took about nineteen hours for the Kennedy administration to pressure Greyhound to provide a driver. After a rumor surfaced that the federal government was going to fly an African American soldier to the city to drive the vehicle, a Greyhound driver was suddenly found."[59] Patterson also promised Kennedy that the riders would be protected from further violence while in Alabama.

Mob Action at the Depot

The bus finally left Birmingham on May 20, nearly one week after the Mother's Day riot and violence. It was part of a long convoy; the bus was accompanied by FBI observers, plainclothes state detectives, highway patrol drivers, and airplanes. Bringing up the rear were hundreds of reporters. But about 40 miles (64km) outside the city of Montgomery, all signs of protection disappeared.

When the riders arrived at the bus station in Montgomery, the depot appeared to be quiet and deserted. Lewis had been chosen to speak for the group, and he was the first one to get off the bus. He describes what happened next:

People came out of nowhere—men, women, children with baseball bats, clubs, chains—and there was no police official around. They just started beating people. . . . Then the mob turned on members of the press. One cameraman . . . had one of these heavy old pieces of camera equipment on his shoulder. This member of the mob took the equipment, bashed this guy, knocked him down, bashed his face in. So they beat up all of the reporters.[60]

The Klan attacked the press first because they and Montgomery officials wanted as few recordings of what was happening as possible. Historian Derek Charles Catsam elaborates: "Many members of the attacking crowd must have taken great pleasure in laying their vengeance upon a group of people who represented the institutions that had made Alabama look like brutal, animalistic, bullying thugs. And so they attacked the unarmed media members before getting to the . . . Freedom Riders."[61]

After the press corps had been beaten, the mob then turned to the riders. Zwerg, one of the white riders, was one of the first targets. As he got off the bus and saw the mob, Zwerg knelt to pray for the courage to remain nonviolent. When he tried to stand, he was grabbed by the mob and kicked in the back; the blows broke three of his vertebrae. A dozen men then surrounded him and began beating him. One man pinned Zwerg's head between his knees so that the others could take turns hitting him. The mob, calling Zwerg a "n———-lover,"[62] knocked out one tooth after another.

Witness Lucretia Collins, one of the riders, described the attack on Zwerg: "Some men held him while white women clawed his face with their nails. And they held up their little children—children who couldn't have been more than a couple years old—to claw his face. I had to turn my head because I just couldn't watch it."[63] Zwerg would spend four days in the hospital before returning home to Wisconsin with a severe concussion, a broken nose, a broken thumb, more than half his teeth fractured, and three cracked vertebrae.

William Barbee, another rider, also came under attack; one Klansman jammed a jagged pipe into his ear, while another hit Barbee in the head with a baseball bat. The beating left Barbee paralyzed.

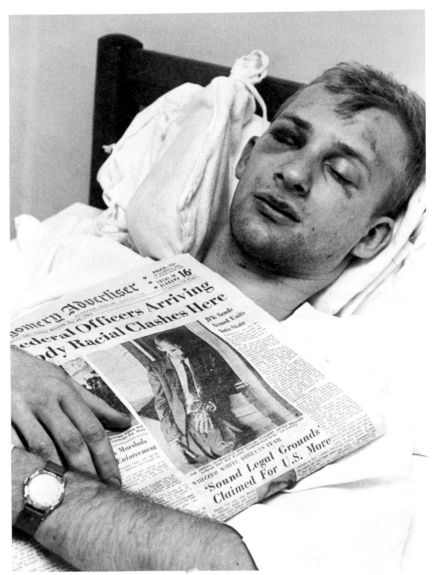

Freedom Rider Jim Zwerg lies in a hospital following an attack by a pro-segregation white mob. He holds a newspaper describing the attack.

John Doar, a member of the Civil Rights Division of the Justice Department, saw what was happening in Montgomery from a building across the street from the station. He immediately called Robert Kennedy and emotionally reported: "The passengers are coming off. A bunch of men . . . are beating them. There are no

61

Diane Nash

Diane Nash was born in Chicago, Illinois; attended Howard University in Washington, D.C.; and later transferred to Fisk University in Nashville, Tennessee. In Nashville she encountered segregation for the first time when she visited the Tennessee State Fair. When she saw the signs for segregated restrooms, she felt immediate humiliation and anger. She would later date her involvement in the civil rights movement to that moment.

At age twenty-two, she became the unofficial leader of the Nashville sit-ins, during which she gained publicity and national attention when she confronted Mayor Ben West and forced him to admit that segregated lunch counters were wrong and immoral. During the Freedom Rides, Nash helped organize and enlist young students to join the rides when they faltered.

Nash also worked with the Southern Christian Leadership Conference (SCLC) from 1961 to 1965. In 1962, although four months pregnant, she was sentenced to two years in prison for teaching nonviolent tactics to schoolchildren in Jackson, Mississippi. She helped design the strategy for the Selma, Alabama, civil rights march and was appointed by President John F. Kennedy to serve on a national committee that eventually led to the passage of the Civil Rights Act of 1964. Historians Lydia McNeill and Robyn Spencer summarize: "She has maintained an unwavering commitment to black empowerment." In 2003 she received the Distinguished American Award from the John F. Kennedy Library.

Lydia McNeill and Robyn Spencer. "Diane Nash." In *Encyclopedia of African American Culture and History*, edited by Colin A. Palmer. New York: Macmillan Reference USA, 2006.

cops. It's terrible. It's terrible. There's not a cop in sight. . . . It's awful."[64] The mob eventually grew to over one thousand, and still there was no sign of any police.

Police Inaction

Seigenthaler, Robert Kennedy's personal representative from the Justice Department who had stationed himself across the street from the depot, was also watching the attack. When he saw two white female riders being attacked and knocked unconscious by several white mob members, he went to their rescue in his car. As he stopped to help the women, he was pulled from his car by Klan members and beaten unconscious with a lead pipe.

Also attacked were dozens of innocent bystanders. The mob poured kerosene on one man and then lit a match, burning him severely. Other injuries were inflicted on over twenty blacks who happened to be nearby.

The mob continued its attack on the riders until Floyd Mann, the director of public safety in Alabama, appeared and fired a shot in the air from his revolver. As one member of the mob attempted to swing a baseball bat at a fallen victim, Mann put his gun next to the man's ear and yelled: "One more swing, and you're dead."[65] Because of his actions that day, Mann is credited with saving the lives of several of the riders. He did so with no support or legal authority. Seigenthaler later reflected on why Mann had stepped in: "Mann's view of police work was, for an Alabama law man in that era, amazingly color blind, and he had been made uneasy by the hate which had begun to swirl through Alabama in the late 1950s, and by the rise of the Klan, operating all too often with local cops."[66]

As the Klansmen and others had carried out the beatings, the police had stood nearby, doing nothing. Tom Lankford of the *Birmingham News* reported: "There was no effort to detain or arrest anyone involved in the beatings. I saw whites and negroes beaten unmercifully while law officers calmly directed traffic."[67]

When questioned later about why the police had not intervened, Montgomery police superintendent L.B. Sullivan responded: "Providing police protection for agitators is not our policy, but we would have been ready if we had had definite and positive information they were coming."[68] However, personal accounts indicated that this statement did not reflect the truth of the matter. Judge Richard Rives, an observer, overheard a local Klansman remark: "Sully [Sullivan] kept his word. He said he'd give us half an hour to beat up those [activists] and he did."[69]

Aftermath

The violence at Montgomery had lasted only fifteen minutes but had left dozens injured and bloody. When the mob finally dispersed, the parking lot at the bus station looked like a battlefield. The pavement was covered with blood and the prostrate bodies of the injured.

Meanwhile, Sullivan was telling local reporters that all the city ambulances were out of service with mechanical breakdowns and thus could not take any of the injured riders to the hospital. Many of the riders were finally taken to hospitals by black church members who had been dispatched by Shuttlesworth. In all, over twenty people needed medical treatment, including four reporters. Only St. Jude's Catholic Hospital would treat any of the riders.

White supremacists in Montgomery were sure that they had stopped the rides once and for all, but it was soon apparent that the riders were not finished. After he regained consciousness, Zwerg told reporters: "We will continue our journey one way or another. We are prepared to die."[70] Zwerg's statement was broadcast on

Freedom Riders stage a sit-in in the Montgomery bus depot's whites-only section. Outside, white citizens attacked riders, sending many to hospitals.

national television. Dozens of new riders, recruited by the SNCC and the Southern Christian Leadership Conference (SCLC), hurried to Montgomery to replace the injured protesters. Hundreds of other people, black and white, northerners and southerners, young and old, were inspired by Zwerg's courage and in the next several weeks volunteered to join the Freedom Rides.

The Kennedy Response

Robert Kennedy was furious when he heard about the violence at the Montgomery bus depot. He believed that Patterson had broken his promise of providing protection for the riders. Kennedy was particularly enraged that Seigenthaler, his personal representative, had been attacked. Journalist and historian David Halberstam explains: "From the moment that John Seigenthaler was knocked unconscious, the struggle became infinitely more personal for Robert Kennedy. . . . His attitude changed overnight to one of cold anger."[71]

After the Montgomery incident, Kennedy also learned that all three attacks in Alabama—Anniston, Birmingham, and Montgomery—had been the work of the Ku Klux Klan. His anger increased when he learned that the FBI, through its undercover agents, had known of the attacks in advance and had done nothing to prevent them.

President John Kennedy was also unhappy about the ongoing violence. The news from Montgomery came shortly before the president was to meet Soviet leader Nikita Khrushchev in Vienna, Austria, to talk about the nuclear arms race. Historian Taylor Branch elaborates: "To face Khrushchev against the backdrop of racial strife within the bosom of the free world . . . would open Kennedy to ridicule from the Soviet leader."[72]

In order to defuse the situation, the president decided to send U.S. Marshals into Alabama. After the violence in Montgomery and what Robert Kennedy saw as a personal attack on one of his assistants, the Kennedys felt that they could no longer trust Patterson to provide protection. Historian Raymond Arsenault explains the president's decision to send in marshals: "The force of federal marshals . . . was the only available deterrent to continued disorder and disrespect. . . . He simply could not allow the image and moral authority of the United States to be undercut by a mob of racist vigilantes."[73]

Montgomery Church Siege

As the marshals were being dispatched, the Freedom Riders were being sheltered in the homes of black activists. The next evening, May 21, they were driven to the First Baptist Church in Montgomery for a large gathering that would include CORE director Farmer, as well as the Reverend Martin Luther King Jr. and several other noteworthy civil rights leaders. The purpose of the gathering was to celebrate the riders and what they had accomplished and also to lend support to the riders and discuss the future. These leaders had all agreed that the larger civil rights movement needed to respond in a positive and outspoken manner. By sunset the church was jammed with over fifteen hundred people, including members of the press.

Outside, a large white mob gathered and continued to grow. This mob, estimated at over one thousand participants, soon had the riders and the congregation trapped inside the church, fearful that any attempt to leave would result in their being attacked. The only thing standing between the mob and the congregants was a dozen U.S. marshals.

It was soon apparent that the marshals would be unable to control the mob. They could not prevent the crowd from throwing rocks and bricks at the church, which broke many of the windows. Crudely made Molotov cocktails—bottles filled with gasoline and lit with a match so they would explode—were also hurled at the church. A car in the parking lot was set on fire. As fear and anxiety grew among those in the church, their children were moved quickly downstairs to the basement, where it was safer.

With the white mob increasing in size and volatility, King was on the phone trying to pressure the attorney general to do more to protect them, since it had become obvious that the marshals could not hold the crowd away. A call went out to Byron White, the deputy attorney general, who promised that more marshals were on the way. When the additional marshals, many of them recently deputized and untrained, arrived, they began to lob tear gas into the crowd in the hopes of dispersing it. Most of the gas, however, made its way into the church, choking the congregation and filling the church with noxious fumes.

With the marshals unable to exert control, Robert Kennedy placed army troops at nearby Fort Benning, Georgia, on alert. He

On May 21, 1961, the congregation in Montgomery's First Baptist Church applauds the presence of Freedom Riders. Outside, racist mobs throw rocks and Molotov cocktails while police watch.

was on the verge of calling his brother, the president, to ask for military reinforcements when he received word that Patterson had declared a state of martial law and was sending in members of the Alabama National Guard.

To the activists, however, the National Guard, rather than dispelling the mob, seemed more intent on containing those trapped inside the church. Around midnight, with the mob kept back by the National Guard, many of the church members began to move toward the door, hoping to go home. The doors, however, were blocked by troops. Lewis describes the scene: "The troops, which had been facing the crowd across the street, now turned to face us. . . . Those soldiers didn't look like protectors now. Their rifles [with bayonets drawn] were pointed our way. They looked like the enemy."[74] Denied their exit, the congregation settled in for the night, scattered on the church floors and pews.

It was not until 4:30 in the morning, after more troops arrived, that the worshippers and activists were finally able to leave the church and return home. The siege was over. The fact that no deaths or injuries occurred was viewed by many of the congregation and the press as a miracle.

The Journey Will Continue

Martial law was still in effect in the city of Montgomery the next morning. Most of the riders, as well as King, Nash, and Farmer, were secluded in the home of Montgomery civil rights activist Richard Harris. Also gathered in Montgomery was a large contingent of media representatives. The press kept asking if the ride would continue. The activists finally issued a response. King spoke for the group on May 23, stating that the ride would proceed into the state of Mississippi.

When Robert Kennedy heard this, he was both furious and alarmed that the rides were continuing. He sent a message to King, asking King and the riders for a cooling-down period before the riders continued. It was Farmer who responded, instructing King: "Please tell the Attorney General that we have been cooling off for three hundred and fifty years. If we cool off any more, we will be in a deep freeze. The Freedom Ride will go on."[75]

After the decision was made to continue the Freedom Ride, Nash immediately sent appeals to other civil rights organizations

The Role of Martin Luther King Jr.

When Martin Luther King Jr., the leading voice in civil rights activism, arrived in Montgomery, Alabama, after the violence at the bus depot, he assumed a position of leadership. King's assumption that he was in charge met with dissatisfaction from many of the students and Freedom Riders. Diane Nash, in particular, was extremely irritated. She believed that it had been the young people who had kept the Freedom Rides going despite the dangers and violence they had faced and endured. She was furious that she was not even being consulted about the future of the rides.

When King refused to accompany the riders on their trip to Mississippi, many of the riders and other civil rights leaders became angry again. Civil rights activist Robert Williams, for instance, sent a telegram to King: "The cause of human decency and black liberation demands that you physically ride the buses. . . . No sincere leader asks his followers to make sacrifices that he himself will not endure. You are a phony." More importantly, King's refusal to join the rides created a schism between King and the students.

Quoted in Raymond Arsenault. *Freedom Riders: 1961 and the Struggle for Racial Justice.* New York: Oxford University Press, 2006, p. 251.

In Montgomery, Martin Luther King Jr. (center, in striped tie) and others greet Freedom Riders as they board a bus.

for more volunteers. James Lawson, who had taught the Nashville students about nonviolence, headed to Montgomery to join the ride. The SNCC and CORE both sent volunteers, and Farmer decided to rejoin the ride. Although declining to join the riders, King was at the depot to watch the riders depart from Montgomery.

The Freedom Riders, riding on two buses, left Montgomery surrounded by guards and police officers who would accompany the riders to Jackson, Mississippi. The riders, although determined to proceed, were anxious. None of them was quite sure what kind of reception awaited them in Mississippi.

Chapter Five

The Arrests

The twenty-seven riders who departed from Montgomery, Alabama, on two buses had every reason to be concerned about what would happen when they reached Mississippi. While Alabama had a long history of racial violence, Mississippi's reputation was even worse. African Americans were frequently jailed for crimes they did not commit and often lynched or murdered by white crowds without benefit of a trial. The state, in fact, led the nation in lynching. It was also the home of the White Citizens' Council, a hate group that used economic and political pressure to preserve racial inequality.

As a rider on one of the buses heading toward Jackson, Mississippi, James Farmer later described the trip: "That ride from Montgomery to Jackson was like a military operation. . . . As we rode the bus, there were Alabama National Guardsmen . . . there were helicopters . . . there were police cars . . . there were federal, state, and county police."[76] There were nearly one thousand National Guardsmen stationed along the 140-mile route (225km) to Mississippi. Mississippi National Guardsmen took over at the state line and accompanied the bus into the bus depot in Jackson. Despite the presence of the National Guard, the riders were expecting a violent welcome.

Anxious about the probable violence, the riders nonetheless felt that it was essential to enter the state and confront segregation there. Their determination to go to Mississippi did not lessen the riders' fears as they approached the city of Jackson on May 24, 1961. They eased their fear by singing: "I'm taking a ride on the Greyhound bus line, I'm riding the front seat to Jackson this time. Hallelujah, I'm a-traveling, Hallelujah, ain't it fine. Hallelujah, I'm a-traveling down freedom's main line."[77]

Armed members of the National Guard accompany Freedom Riders to Jackson, Mississippi. Nearly one thousand guardsmen lined the route from Montgomery to Jackson.

Arrest

The activists were surprised by the welcome they received in Jackson: There was no mob waiting at the depot. Robert Kennedy, in a move that the riders knew nothing about, had made a deal with

Mississippi authorities. He negotiated an end to the violence with Mississippi senator James O. Eastland, chair of the Senate Judiciary Committee and a powerful voice in Washington, D.C. Eastland, a committed white supremacist, promised Kennedy that there would be no violence in Mississippi in exchange for Kennedy's agreement that the riders would be arrested upon their arrival in Jackson. Kennedy made this deal knowing that the riders had done nothing to warrant such an arrest. Historian Raymond Arsenault elaborates: "In effect, the rioting in Alabama had

Upon their arrival in Jackson, Mississippi, Freedom Riders were immediately arrested. Hoping to avoid continued mob violence, U.S. attorney general Robert Kennedy did not dispute the arrests.

convinced the Kennedy brothers . . . that almost anything was preferable to mob violence—including unconstitutional arrests."[78]

When the bus pulled into the Jackson depot, the riders were met by officers from the Jackson city police. One of the riders, Fred Leonard, describes the scene: "We never got stopped. They [the police] passed us right on through the white terminal, into the paddy wagon, and into jail."[79]

All twenty-seven riders were arrested that day on charges of trespassing and breach of peace and taken to jail. They went to court 2 days later and were given a two-hundred-dollar fine and a suspended 60-day sentence. The riders refused bail, and several of them launched a hunger strike. Because they had refused to pay the fine, the authorities determined that they would remain in jail for a period of 60 days. After three days in a Jackson jail, they were transferred to Hinds County Prison Farm, where they were crammed into small jail cells for two weeks. While in jail the prisoners learned that hundreds of other riders were arriving in Jackson on a daily basis. As these riders arrived, they, too, were arrested. Over the summer, over three hundred riders would be arrested in Jackson and serve time in prison.

After three weeks at the county prison farm, the riders found out they were being transferred because of overcrowding at the jail and prison farm. On June 15, 1961, the riders were taken to the Mississippi State Penitentiary, also known as Parchman Farm. Parchman had a reputation among blacks in Mississippi and was nearly synonymous with brutality and violence. Award-winning novelist William Faulkner, a native of Mississippi, referred to Parchman in one of his novels as "Destination Doom."[80] Every African American in the South, in fact, knew about the reputation of Parchman Farm.

Parchman Farm

The riders received a harsh welcome to the prison and felt that the intention of the authorities at Parchman was to break their spirit and put a stop to the rides. John Lewis describes the riders' first few hours at Parchman:

> We were led into a cement building where deputies with cattle prods stood by while we were ordered to strip naked.

For two and a half hours we stood wearing nothing. . . . I could see that this was an attempt to break us down, to humiliate and dehumanize us, to rob us of our identity and self-worth. . . . This was 1961 in America, yet here we were, treated like animals for using the wrong bathroom.[81]

At Parchman, the riders were beyond the legal help of the Congress of Racial Equality (CORE), the National Association for the Advancement of Colored People (NAACP), and the federal government. They were at the mercy of the warden and guards, who seemed to be intent on making their lives as difficult as possible. Once inside the prison, the riders were each given a Bible, an aluminum cup, and a toothbrush. These were their only possessions. Equipped with a toilet, sink, and bunk bed, the small cells measured only 6 feet by 8 feet (1.8m by 2.4m). A lightbulb on the ceiling was kept on twenty-four hours a day. The prisoners were separated from one another by the walls of their cells.

The prisoners were also denied even a few minutes outside for exercise. When Farmer asked for the group to be allowed outside, prison superintendent Fred Jones responded: "We ain't goin' to let y'all go no place. . . . We've got to feed ya, but we can put so much salt in y' food that y' won't be able to eat it."[82] The following week, the superintendent followed through with this threat, ordering the kitchen to lace the prisoners' food with mounds of salt.

The Freedom Riders later reported experiencing a variety of hardships and abuses while in prison. Former Freedom Riders described what the prisoners experienced, saying: "The Riders . . . [had to] endure poisonous hatred, inedible food, and vicious beatings. Fire hoses . . . [were] used to smash bodies against the steel bars, and the prisoners . . . [were] tortured with agonizing electric cattle prods."[83] One of the student activists, Stokely Carmichael, later described what the prods felt like: "When the prod touched your skin, the pain was sharp and excruciating, at once a jolting shock and a burn. You could see puffs of smoke and smell the odor of roasting flesh."[84]

The female prisoners had to deal with sexual indignities in addition to poor living conditions. Female prison matrons gave them brutal and painful vaginal examinations, and male guards watched them shower and dress. California rider Janice Rogers

Punishment for Singing

———◼———

To keep up their spirits while at Parchman Farm, the riders sang their freedom songs. David B. Fankhauser, a white rider from Ohio, describes the experience: "Without a doubt, spirited singing of these songs were the high point of our experience at Parchman. . . . Our singing went on for hours and hours a day."

When a guard threatened them that he would take away their toothbrushes if they did not stop singing, the prisoners only sang louder. Fankhauser elaborates: "We sang louder. Out went toothbrushes. We kept singing. He ordered that our Bibles be taken; we sang louder. If we didn't stop singing he would have our mattresses and bedding taken out. We sang with even more gusto."

When the riders still refused to stop their singing, the guards then removed the screens on the jail cell windows. This allowed hordes of mosquitoes into the prison. Fankhauser explains:

> A guard came in and said, "Wow look at all them bugs. We're gonna have to spray!" Shortly thereafter, we heard what sounded like a large diesel truck pull up outside . . . and what looked like a fire hose was passed in through one of the big windows. As the engine powered up outside, we were hit with a powerful spray of DDT [a toxic insecticide]. Being trapped in our cells with no protection, our bodies and every inch of our cells were drenched with eye-stinging, skin-burning insecticide.

David B. Fankhauser. "Freedom Rides." Freedom Ride. http://biology.clc.uc.edu/Fankhauser/Society/freedom_ride/Freedom_Ride_DBF.htm.

At Mississippi's notorious Parchman Prison Farm, Freedom Riders endured many indignities at the hands of their white jailers.

suffered a miscarriage when her request for medical attention was ignored. Rider Theresa Walker later described the county jail cell where a number of the female riders were imprisoned: "They gave us dirty mattresses and we put them on the floor. If you woke up at night you would see the bugs crawling over the other girls. It was terrible."[85]

Survival and Release

On July 7, 1961, three weeks and one day after their arrival at Parchman, the prisoners were released. Despite the brutality and isolation, all 328 of the riders survived.

Each rider, as he or she exited the prison, felt that the riders had accomplished something. Black activist and rider C.T. Vivian explains: "The feeling of people coming out of the jail was one that they had triumphed, that they had achieved, that they were now ready, they could go back home, they could be a witness to a new understanding. Nonviolence was proven. . . . It had become a national movement."[86]

As the riders walked out of the prison's gates, they were met by a small group of lawyers and friends. There was no press contingent present. In fact, once the riders were in prison, the media had been unable to gain entrance or get updates on the prisoners. The riders had been allowed no visitors. An exception was made for two representatives from Minnesota, who were granted access to Parchman but were allowed only a brief and tightly monitored visit with two riders from that state. The representatives were given a very limited tour of the facilities and left the prison believing the riders were being treated humanely. The truth was known only after the riders were released and began to talk to the press.

A Legal Battle

Prison had placed a huge financial burden on CORE, which was continuing to bear the primary responsibility for the riders. Each rider had to pay a five-hundred-dollar bond at the end of his or her initial time in jail; this was required in order for an appeal to be made when the cases went to trial. Lawyers wanted the riders' cases to go to trial so that they could later appeal the arrests as unconstitutional. They were all still facing charges of trespassing, breach of peace, and disorderly conduct.

Civil rights activist the Reverend C.T. Vivian, center, was jailed in Parchman, along with other Freedom Riders. Upon being released, Vivian and the others felt they had triumphed in demonstrating the impact of nonviolence.

This was the first of many financial impacts on the organization. CORE also wanted to provide each rider with a defense attorney as well as transportation back home. The average cost for each rider soon reached over one thousand dollars. With more than three hundred riders imprisoned, the financial impact was enormous.

Media Exposure: Critical and Complimentary

During the later stages of the Freedom Rides, several major magazines did complimentary cover stories on the riders. *Time* magazine, for instance, featured a five-page article titled "The South and the Freedom Riders." In the article, the authors did profiles of Diane Nash, James Lawson, and James Farmer, among others. *Life* magazine published ten pages of photographs. The only magazine that portrayed the riders in a negative light was the conservative *National Review*; authors in this magazine defended segregation.

Despite the positive articles, there were also signs that many Americans were getting tired of hearing about the rides. The *New York Times* called for a cooling-off period in an editorial, writing that the Freedom Riders had proved their case. Many Americans were also concerned that the rides would cause widespread social disorder and riots.

Another critic was David Brinkley, a native of North Carolina. On the *NBC Evening News*, Brinkley editorialized that "the Freedom Riders are accomplishing nothing whatsoever and, on the contrary, are doing positive harm."

Quoted in Raymond Arsenault. *Freedom Riders: 1961 and the Struggle for Racial Justice*. New York: Oxford University Press, 2006, p. 289.

CORE therefore had to rely on personal loans and large donations to manage the financial responsibility for the riders.

All of the riders were required to return to Jackson on August 14, 1961, in order to be arraigned, or charged with the crimes for which they had been arrested. Judge Russell Moore of Mississippi began the hearings on August 22, 1961. Defense attorneys immediately asked that the riders be tried in a class action suit, so that they could all be tried together. Since all of the riders were charged with the same crime, a class action suit could be tried quickly and would be less expensive for CORE. The judge immediately refused the request. Mississippi officials intended to drag out the trials as long as possible using every method available. Determined to stop the Freedom Rides and the momentum of the civil rights movement, the officials hoped to exhaust the financial resources of the civil rights organizations. Nearly three hundred riders would be tried separately during the next year.

Hank Thomas, a young black student, was the first rider to go to trial. Moore ruled immediately that the *Boynton* decision, mandating desegregated interstate facilities, was irrelevant to the case. The all-white jury deliberated only forty-five minutes before returning with a guilty verdict on a charge of disturbing the peace. Thomas was sentenced to four months in jail. The other trials ended in the same quick manner and with an identical sentence. Many riders served the full prison sentence; others paid their two-hundred-dollar fine and an additional three dollars a day for time in jail they did not serve.

There was little media coverage of the trials, which lasted through late May 1962. The NAACP legal team later appealed all the convictions and took the cases before the Supreme Court. The Supreme Court eventually had all of riders' court records expunged and their sentences reversed in 1965.

The same day that Thomas was sentenced, the governor of Alabama, John Patterson, signed a state law that called for jail terms and fines for any riders still in Alabama. Judge Frank Johnson of Alabama also issued a restraining order that prohibited any civil rights organization from conducting any Freedom Ride through the state of Alabama. This did not deter Freedom Riders, who found other routes into the South.

More Rides Take Place

Despite the arrests, prison sentences, and trials, Freedom Riders on dozens of buses were still flooding into the South from all over the United States. New recruits were coming in constantly, especially from the North. One set of northern riders included Yale University chaplain and activist William Sloane Coffin Jr., along with other clergy and university officials. They joined the ride, Coffin explained, to let the nation know that the rides were not just a student movement. The group also hoped to encourage southern moderates and clergypeople to speak out against racism.

The rides continued into June, July, August, and September 1961. Virtually every day brought at least one new group of riders to Jackson. More than sixty different rides crisscrossed the

Freedom Riders eat at the Greyhound bus station in Tallahassee, Florida in June 1961. Unlike this peaceful event, riders at a nearby airport restaurant were refused service and later arrested for "unlawful assembly."

South, the majority of them converging on Jackson, where, without exception, the riders were arrested and jailed.

Elsewhere, some of the riders encountered problems, such as an incident that occurred in Tallahassee, Florida. A group of interfaith riders was at the airport and preparing to fly home to Washington, D.C., when the riders attempted to eat at a terminal restaurant. Airport officials, rather than serving them, decided to close the restaurant. In the meantime a large crowd of angry white protesters had arrived. When a Tallahassee city attorney ordered the riders to leave and the riders refused, the riders were arrested for unlawful assembly. At trial, they were given the choice between thirty days in jail or a five-hundred-dollar fine. Most chose the jail term.

Support for the Freedom Rides

As the momentum of the Freedom Rides continued to grow, support came from a wide variety of sources. The entire civil rights movement, for example, began to voice support for the riders. Even Roy Wilkins, the director of the NAACP and a one-time critic of the rides, lined up behind the riders. He urged the student members of over one hundred NAACP college chapters to insist on desegregated travel when they returned home.

High school students and other young people in Jackson, Mississippi, also decided to join the fight against segregated interstate buses. The students, largely as a result of Martin Luther King Jr.'s encouragement, formed the Jackson Non-Violent Movement and appeared at a Greyhound bus station where they, too, were promptly arrested. Young people in other areas of the South joined the fight by taking similar actions.

The rides were also garnering support from a wide variety of Americans. In New York the noted Broadway team of Elaine May and Mike Nichols hosted a benefit for the riders. Support also came from New York governor Nelson Rockefeller, whose son-in-law was a Freedom Rider.

In addition, in September 1961 ABC aired the program *Walk in My Shoes*, which for the first time portrayed segregation from the standpoint of African Americans. And in Washington, D.C., more than one hundred pro-riders demonstrated in front of the White House.

The Freedom Ride Coordinating Committee

———————————■———————————

The Freedom Ride Coordinating Committee (FRCC) was established on May 26, 1961, by Martin Luther King Jr. and other civil rights activists. The purpose of the committee was to recruit and send volunteers to join the Freedom Rides in the South. The group established recruitment centers throughout the South and other parts of the country and also initiated fund-raising efforts to finance more rides.

Hundreds of volunteers joined the rides as a result of the committee's efforts, enabling the rides to continue throughout the summer of 1961. These new riders also challenged other forms of discrimination by sitting together in segregated restaurants and hotels.

The FRCC also kept the riders' movement in the public eye by doing press conferences as well as radio and television interviews. Many of the riders were involved in these interviews, giving firsthand accounts of what they had encountered in the South.

Thanks in large part to the FRCC, the total number of riders who participated in the rides grew to 436. Of those, 75 percent were male and 75 percent of the total riders were under age thirty. Whites and blacks were equally divided. The riders were also one of the most diverse groups of protestors to act during the civil rights era. Riders came from all over the United States and from every walk of life.

White endorsement of the Freedom Rides in the South, however, was rare. One exception was Ralph McGill, the editor of the *Atlanta Constitution*, who wrote: "The real agitators are the states involved especially those that tolerate political demagoguery [appealing to prejudices] and mob action."[87] Most southerners, however, continued to condemn the rides.

The average American was also not supportive of the Freedom Riders. In a June 21, 1961, Gallup poll, only 24 percent of Americans approved of the rides, while 70 percent disapproved. While 61 percent favored desegregation in the future, only 23 percent favored it immediately. This lack of support was most visible in the absence of articles about the riders in the majority of newspapers across the United States. The riders were making front-page news only in Mississippi and Alabama.

Despite the lack of support from average Americans and the absence of media coverage, the riders were moving forward. So, too, was the federal government.

Chapter Six

Impact and Reflections

By the time the Freedom Rides ended in late 1961, several hundred riders had used interstate buses to travel throughout the South. Many of these riders would continue their commitment to ending segregation by playing leading roles in future civil rights actions. And, as a direct result of the Freedom Rides and the ongoing southern resistance and violence, along with increasing pressure and demands from civil rights leaders, the federal government was finally compelled to act.

The Justice Department Takes Action

As the end of May 1961 approached, hundreds of Freedom Riders were still streaming into the South. As they, too, were arrested, Parchman Farm began to swell with those who had been imprisoned. Even while the first waves of Freedom Riders were still imprisoned, pressure from civil rights leaders mounted on the federal government to take action to protect future riders.

Partly as a result of this pressure, on May 29, 1961, Attorney General Robert Kennedy announced that he was asking the Interstate Commerce Commission (ICC) to enforce the Supreme Court decisions relating to interstate bus travel. With this announcement, the attorney general was making it clear that his department would no longer allow the law to be ignored. Kennedy, in a statement released to the press, told the ICC: "The time has come for this commission to declare unequivocally by regulation that a Negro passenger is free to travel the length of this country in the same manner as any other passenger."[88]

The ICC had been created in 1887 to regulate railroad travel. The Motor Carrier Act of 1935 had increased the ICC's responsibility to include interstate buses. The commission set regulations for the entire interstate transportation system and could impose fines or revoke the license of companies that did not comply with the rules. In the years that had passed, however, nothing had been done to prevent discrimination on bus lines, despite two Supreme Court rulings. The ICC began internal arguments and discussions on Kennedy's request on August 15, 1961.

In late June the Justice Department had also made another eventful decision. For the first time the federal government went to court to challenge segregation; in this case in the air terminal

U.S. attorney general Robert Kennedy announced on May 29, 1961, that his department would no longer allow the Supreme Court's ruling on interstate bus travel to be ignored and that the Interstate Commerce Commission must enforce the law.

facilities in New Orleans. Older airports had complicated leasing arrangements with a number of airlines that tended to place the segregation that occurred in their restaurants out of reach of the federal government. Because the New Orleans airport was new, the federal government hoped to use this case as a test case for integration. On June 26 the Justice Department filed suit to end segregation at New Orleans International Airport.

The ICC Issues a Decision

While the Justice Department was pursuing its case in New Orleans, the ICC was meeting to discuss integrating interstate bus transportation. On September 1, 1961, the commission issued a unanimous decision that prohibited racial discrimination in interstate bus transportation. Beginning on the first of November, the commission announced, all buses would be required to post signs that stated: "Seating aboard this vehicle is without regard to race, color, creed, or national origin."[89] The decision would also apply to bus terminals and terminal restaurants, but not to train or air travel. Each violation would be punishable by a fine of five hundred dollars. The decision was received with praise from the national press, but many southern leaders announced they would not heed it.

CORE officials, upon learning of the ICC decision, immediately announced that the organization would begin sending out teams of riders on November 1 to test whether the new law was being enforced. The teams found that the states of West Virginia, Virginia, Kentucky, and Texas were, for the most part, complying with the regulation. In Louisiana, Florida, North and South Carolina, and Georgia, there were numerous violations, but in Mississippi and Alabama, the law was still being flagrantly ignored. In the southern Mississippi town of Taylorsville, for instance, a police officer shot and killed Corporal Roman Duckworth after the young black soldier refused to move to the back of the bus. The police officer was not charged with any offense. Historian Raymond Arsenault elaborates: "In Southern bus terminals, as in other areas of regional life, old ways died hard even in the face of a federal mandate."[90]

Yet in many places in the South, interstate bus travelers of all races were finally sitting together on buses without the risk of arrest. The "Whites Only" and "Colored" signs from depot restrooms and lunch counters had largely disappeared. In all, over eighty-five transportation terminals in the South were successfully desegregated. By the end of 1962, CORE reported that the battle had been won against segregated travel on interstate bus lines. James Farmer announced: "We put on pressure and create a crisis and then they react. I am absolutely convinced that the ICC order wouldn't have been issued were it not for the Freedom Riders."[91]

The Riders Move Forward

In the years that followed the Freedom Rides, most of the riders went their separate ways. Many of them had distinguished careers in education, politics, and the ministry. For instance, Rodney Powell and Gloria Johnson, two young black medical students from Nashville, Tennessee, went on to become two of the first doctors chosen for the Peace Corps in Africa. Bernard Lafayette, an African American student at American Baptist College in Nashville, would become that school's president many years later.

A few riders later sued the federal government for damages incurred during the Freedom Rides. James Peck and Walter Bergman, both severely injured during the rides, filed separate civil suits against the FBI. They both charged the FBI with negligence in not intervening to stop the violence. Peck was eventually awarded twenty-five thousand dollars in damages, while Bergman received fifty thousand dollars.

Dozens of riders were kept busy with speaking engagements at colleges and other venues in the North and Midwest. Many riders planned to continue their education. Some were able to do so, though a few encountered problems. Fourteen riders at Tennessee State University, for instance, were expelled for participating in the rides.

Many of the Freedom Riders would also play very active roles in later civil rights events. John Lewis, for example, spoke from the Lincoln Memorial during the March on Washington in 1963 and later participated in Bloody Sunday in 1965, when six hundred civil rights workers were beaten by police wielding clubs in Selma, Alabama. Lewis later wrote of his long-term commitment to the civil rights movement: "If there was anything I learned on that long, bloody bus trip of 1961, it was this—that we were in for a long, bloody fight here in the American South. And I intended to be in the middle of it."[92]

The Impact of the Rides: Youth Movement

In 1966 militant activist Stokely Carmichael replaced John Lewis as chair of the SNCC.

Many of the leaders of the civil rights movement came from among the Freedom Riders. The rides, for instance, brought students and the Student Nonviolent Coordinating Committee (SNCC) to the forefront of the civil rights movement. Although not the original leaders of the Freedom Rides, Nashville's student activists and other young people soon became the movement's driving force.

As more and more young people joined the Freedom Rides, however, many of them were not schooled in the technique of nonviolence. Many of them, in fact, wanted instead to meet violence with violence. The youth movement, as a result, became more militant. John Lewis elaborates: "This, it would turn out, would become the most significant result of the Freedom Rides: the turning toward radicalization of the movement, a militancy that would surge and swell month by month over the coming years."

Lewis, in fact, resigned from the SNCC in 1966 because of this very issue. The organization had come under the leadership of Stokely Carmichael, another Freedom Rider—but a man determined to take a more militant stance. Carmichael began using the Black Power symbol, a raised fist, to denote a move toward violence.

John Lewis with Michael D'Orso. *Walking with the Wind: A Memoir of the Movement.* San Diego: Harcourt, Brace, 1999, p. 176.

Diane Nash, who coordinated the student phase of the Freedom Rides, also continued working for civil rights. She was later appointed by John Kennedy to serve on a national committee to prepare the Civil Rights Act, and in 2003 she received the Distinguished American Award from the John F. Kennedy Library. Many other riders were also active in the civil rights movement and later played important roles in the movement for women's rights, the anti–Vietnam War movement, and the fight for gay and lesbian rights.

Many of the riders also formed long-lasting friendships. Journalist and historian David Halberstam describes their closeness: "They were in ways not unlike members of the same infantry unit which has been in combat for well more than a year, in which the bonds of friendship within the unit become stronger than those the members have with any of their family members or previous friends."[93] In fact, many of the riders found it difficult to be with old friends and family after the Freedom Rides. Their experiences made them outsiders because other people could not relate or really understand all that they had been through. California representative

One of the few female leaders in the civil rights movement, Diane Nash, pictured, was later appointed by President Kennedy to serve on a committee that helped pass the Civil Rights Act.

Bob Filner, who joined the Freedom Rides in Birmingham, Alabama, describes how the rides affected his life:

> It gave to all of us an optimism about change in America that if you get involved, work with other people, you can actually change America. . . . You know, we still have racism and discrimination, but we changed the laws in the Southern states. And that optimism about change has always stayed with me. It led me to run for office and be in Congress, that working together with people . . . we can actually change America.[94]

The Impact of the Rides: The Fight Against Segregation

While the Freedom Rides had a tremendous effect on the lives of those who participated, it also had a huge impact on the future of the civil rights movement. *Jet* magazine editors elaborate: "In all there were dozens of Freedom Rides throughout the south in

On February, 7, 2011, former Freedom Rider Reginald Green speaks to a crowd celebrating the fiftieth anniversary of the Freedom Rides. Forty college students were picked to reenact the rides by retracing the original riders' journey through the South.

Anniversaries

◼

Since 1961 there have been many reunions for the Freedom Riders. They have also celebrated many anniversaries. The first was held in 1981, the twentieth anniversary of the rides, when James Farmer and John Lewis hosted a small gathering in Atlanta, Georgia.

The thirtieth anniversary of the Freedom Rides came in 1991. Lewis, a representative from the state of Georgia and an original Freedom Rider, organized the three-day celebration. A partial reenactment of the first Freedom Ride took place when Lewis and other original riders boarded a bus in Atlanta and headed to Alabama. This ride was broadcast live on C-Span. The riders stopped in Anniston and then celebrated their journey at the First Baptist Church in Montgomery, site of the all-night siege in 1961.

May 4, 2011, was the fiftieth anniversary of the start of the Freedom Rides. Forty college students were chosen out of one thousand volunteers to accompany many of the original riders on a fiftieth-anniversary bus journey through the South. Charles Reed Jr., a student at the University of Mary Washington in Virginia, was one of the students invited to participate. He stated: "What the Freedom Rides did fifty years ago paved the way for what I have today as an African-American."[1]

One of the purposes of the anniversary ride was to teach young people about the Freedom Rides. Glenda Gaither Davis, a Freedom Rider, said: "The young people need to know about past struggles so they can solve current and future problems."[2] Freedom Ride coordinator Diane Nash further elaborated: "The lesson from the Freedom Rides is to take the country's future into your own hands."[3]

1. Quoted in Zinie Chen Sampson. "College Students Retrace 1961 Freedom Ride." MSNBC.com, May 7, 2011. www.msnbc.msn.com/id/42943337/ns/us_news-life.
2. Quoted in Sampson. "College Students Retrace 1961 Freedom Ride."
3. Quoted in Sampson. "College Students Retrace 1961 Freedom Ride."

1961 . . . in what became a watershed [moment] in the Civil Rights Movement."[95] The rides brought the plight of black Americans and the harsh inequality of segregation to the public eye. Lewis, one of the riders, explains:

It dramatized the situation of segregation in the South . . . and it forced the federal government to respond. . . . But the real significance of the Freedom Riders went far beyond bus station snack bars and restaurants. The rides marked a shift in the temperature of the movement, an upsurge in our aggressiveness. We were no longer content to simply wait for the government and courts to respond on their own terms and their own timetable.[96]

The Freedom Rides also impacted citizens around the world. Black people in Africa and elsewhere began to protest the conditions in which they lived. In Australia, for instance, the Aborigines, that nation's native people, having been discriminated against for centuries, staged their own freedom ride. United Nations secretary-general U Thant stated in November 1961: "The Freedom Riders journeying to the south are looked upon in Asia and Africa as the Champions for the colored American's holy war of freedom."[97]

The Impact of the Rides: Politics

The Freedom Rides also had an impact on the federal government. Robert Kennedy's action with the ICC was the first step toward more federal involvement in civil rights. The attorney general also urged civil rights activists to work on voting rights throughout the South. By the end of 1961, the Justice Department was playing a more involved role in civil rights matters. In effect, Lisa Cozzens summarizes, "they [the Freedom Riders] forced the Kennedy administration to take a stand on civil rights."[98]

The rides also exposed the weakness of President Kennedy's commitment to civil rights. Prior to the Freedom Rides, Kennedy's primary interest had been foreign policy; he was unprepared to address the issues in the South. Politically, Kennedy was too dependent on southern Democrats in Congress, needing them to get any legislation passed. Kennedy also knew that civil rights legislation would antagonize voters in the South and potentially hurt his chances of reelection in 1964.

The rides made civil rights a pressing national issue, and after many more battles and numerous protests, President Kennedy went before the nation and proposed an extensive civil rights bill. In his speech, Kennedy stated: "A great change is at hand and our task, our obligation is to make that revolution, that change, peaceful and constructive for all. Those who do nothing are inviting shame as well as violence. Those who act boldly are recognizing right as well as reality."[99]

Even after this federal acknowledgement of the need for civil rights legislation, more challenges had to be faced. It would not be until after Kennedy's assassination in November 1963 that President Lyndon Johnson actually introduced the bill giving African Americans full civil rights. The U.S. Congress finally approved the Civil Rights Act in 1964, along with a Voting Rights Act. The Civil Rights Act outlawed discrimination in all aspects of life based on race, sex, color, religion, or national origin, while the Voting Rights Act of 1965 ended discriminatory voting practices.

President Lyndon Johnson, seated, hands Martin Luther King Jr. one of the pens Johnson used to sign the Civil Rights Act. The act outlawed discrimination in all aspects of life based on race, sex, color, religion, and national origin.

The Impact of the Rides: The Press

In addition to impacting politics, the Freedom Rides also changed the way Americans learned about current events. In the past, most Americans relied on newspapers to bring them the news of the previous day. Television, during the Freedom Rides, brought the news into homes with an immediacy and a sense of drama, giving Americans a front-row seat to see what was happening in the South. The image of a bus burning on the road to Anniston, in fact, helped initiate a shift in public opinion. Pictures of well-dressed black men and women being beaten by white mobs in Birmingham and Montgomery, Alabama also made a tremendous impact on the conscience of America.

One of the things that civil rights leaders learned during the Freedom Rides was the importance of the press. These leaders, especially Martin Luther King Jr., would later coordinate all the movement's big protests with an awareness of having television reporters and camera persons on-site. Halberstam elaborates: "Because of the coming of television, events were no longer covered by the press; they were covered by the media; more important, we were going from the use of words to define events to the coming of images to define them."[100] Activists found that images tended to have a much bigger impact on the public than written words.

The Impact of the Rides: A Growing Mass Movement

The courage of the Freedom Riders, as depicted in the media and as viewed by eyewitnesses, inspired thousands of Americans, both black and white. Over the next four years, Americans from every walk of life flooded the South to work on civil rights. Some helped register voters, while others marched to protest racial and political injustice. Ellen Ziskind, a white woman from Massachusetts who was a student at Columbia University in New York, became a Freedom Rider in the latter months of the summer of 1961. She was inspired by the early riders and spoke of the impression they made on her: "They were young. They'd been kicked and beaten and jailed. . . . They were really dedicated to nonviolence. . . . I had never met anybody like them. . . . They believed in democracy in a way I never thought about it. They believed in things I took for

Unusual Reunions

In 2009 Georgia representative and former Freedom Rider John Lewis had an unusual visitor. It was Elwin Wilson, the man who had hit him in Rock Hill, South Carolina, forty-eight years earlier. Wilson had come to apologize. He explained why he felt the need to do so. Wilson stated that when a police officer had asked Lewis if he wanted to press charges against Wilson, Lewis had said no and then stated: "We're not here to cause trouble. We're here for people to love each other." Those words haunted Wilson for forty-eight years. Wilson is the only individual involved in the violence of the rides ever to apologize to Lewis.

In another unusual reunion, Hank Thomas, one of the riders who was badly injured in the Anniston bus bombing, was reunited with the young girl who offered him water as he lay on the side of the road. This reunion occurred on an episode of *The Oprah Winfrey Show* that celebrated the fiftieth anniversary of the Freedom Rides. As Janie Forsyth McKinney was introduced, Thomas gave her a huge hug and called her his little angel. He and other riders credit her with risking her own life to save theirs.

Quoted in *The Oprah Winfrey Show*. "Oprah Honors Freedom Riders." Oprah.com, May 4, 2011. www.oprah.com/oprahshow/Oprah-Honors-Freedom-Riders/8.

In 2009 Congressman John Lewis, a former Freedom Rider, receives an apology from a regretful Elwin Wilson, center, who had participated in a 1961 mob attack on Lewis in Rock Hill, South Carolina.

granted and they were willing to die for it. . . . There was something about them . . . their commitment."[101]

The riders had also impacted southern blacks. Many African Americans had yearned for the day when segregation and prejudice would be challenged. With the Freedom Riders challenging segregation on interstate buses, they were encouraged that steps were finally being taken to end discrimination. Hattye Gatson, a rural resident of the South, stated: "I was working at a private home during the time and would turn on the TV and see all the riots, and I just couldn't wait to get involved."[102] Gatson and hundreds of other blacks began to get involved in not only the Freedom Rides but other civil rights causes that followed.

The Freedom Rides had proved that ordinary citizens could not only affect but change public policy. Lewis elaborates: "The lifeblood of the movement was not going to be the spokesmen . . . but it was going to be the tens of thousands of faceless, anonymous men, women, and children . . . who were going to rise like an irresistible army as this movement for civil rights took shape."[103] These same anonymous citizens would eventually form the backbone of the civil rights protests and actions that would follow the rides. The rides, in fact, had changed the character of the civil rights movement. Utilizing ordinary citizens, especially young people, the movement became more of a mass movement. Arsenault elaborates: "They [the Freedom Riders], more than any other activists of their day, foreshadowed the grassroots rights revolution that would transform American citizenship over the next four decades."[104]

In the years to come, many Americans called the Freedom Riders heroes. Frank Holloway, one of the riders, says he did not feel like a hero: "I can't speak for nobody else, but I know for myself, I felt that this was what I was supposed to do. I didn't feel like I was a hero or anything like that. I just felt that this was what I was supposed to do. And I did it and when I stopped doing it, I didn't feel like anybody needed to reward me or congratulate me or pat me on my back. I did what I felt like I had to do."[105]

Notes

Introduction: A Fight for Integration

1. Quoted in Raymond Arsenault. *Freedom Riders: 1961 and the Struggle for Racial Justice*. New York: Oxford University Press, 2006, p. 145.
2. Quoted in Michel Martin. "Freedom Riders Reflect on 50th Anniversary." National Public Radio, May 4, 2011. www.npr.org/2011/05/04/135985034/freedom-riders-reflect-on-50th-anniversary.
3. Roger Wilkins. "Mission to Dixie." *Washington Post*, January 15, 2006.
4. Quoted in Clayborne Carson, ed. *The Autobiography of Martin Luther King, Jr.* New York: Warner, 1998, p. 153.
5. Quoted in *The Oprah Winfrey Show*. "Oprah Honors Freedom Riders." Oprah.com, May 4, 2011. www.oprah.com/oprahshow/Oprah-Honors-Freedom-Riders/1.

Chapter One: The Jim Crow South

6. Quoted in Eric Etheridge, Roger Wilkins, and Diane McWhorter. *Breach of Peace: Portraits of the 1961 Mississippi Freedom Riders*. New York: Atlas, 2008, p. 15.
7. Quoted in Sanford Wexler. *The Civil Rights Movement: An Eyewitness History*. New York: Facts On File, 1993, p. 22.
8. Vernellia R. Randell. "Examples of Jim Crow Laws." Race, Racism, and the Law. http://academic.udayton.edu/race/02rights/jcrow02.htm.
9. Arsenault. *Freedom Riders*, p. 15.
10. Quoted in *American Experience*. "Freedom Riders." PBS, May 16, 2001. www.pbs.org/wgbh/americanexperience/freedomriders.
11. Quoted in *Star* (South Africa). "Freedom Rider Who Changed Law." August 15, 2007.
12. Lisa Cozzens. "Freedom Rides." Civil Rights Movement, 1955–1965. www.watson.org/~Lisa/blackhistory/civilrights-55-65/freeride.html.
13. Supreme Court of the United States: "Brown v Board of Education 347 US 483 (1954)." *National Center.* http://www.nationalcenter.org/brown.html

Chapter Two: Prelude and Beginnings of the Journey

14. Cozzens. "Freedom Rides."
15. John Lewis with Michael D'Orso. *Walking with the Wind: A Memoir of the Movement*. San Diego: Harcourt Brace, 1999, p. 7.
16. Quoted in Wexler. *The Civil Rights Movement*, p. 109.

17. Herb Boyd. *We Shall Overcome*. Naperville, IL: Sourcebooks, 2004, p. 77.
18. Quoted in Boyd. *We Shall Overcome*, p. 78.
19. Quoted in Boyd. *We Shall Overcome*, p. 85.
20. Benjamin Quarles. *The Negro in the Making of America*. New York: Simon and Schuster, 1996, p. 295.
21. Quoted in Boyd. *We Shall Overcome*, p. 102.
22. David Halberstam. *The Children*. New York, 1998, p. 217.
23. Quoted in Wexler. *The Civil Rights Movement*, p. 128.
24. Quoted in "Boynton v Virginia, 1960." In *Supreme Court Drama: Cases That Changed America*, by Daniel E. Brannen and Richard Clay Hanes. Farmington Hills, MI: UXL, 2001.
25. Jessie Carney Smith and Linda T. Wynn, eds. *Freedom Facts and Firsts: 400 Years of the African American Civil Rights Experience*. Detroit: Visible Ink, 2009, p. 164.
26. Quoted in Henry Hampton and Steve Fayer. *Voices of Freedom: An Oral History of the Civil Rights Movement from the 1950s through the 1980s*. New York: Bantam, 1990, p. 75.
27. Quoted in Boyd. *We Shall Overcome*, p. 90.
28. Quoted in Juan Williams. *Eyes on the Prize: America's Civil Rights Years, 1954–1965*. New York: Viking Penguin, 1987, p. 147.
29. Quoted in Scott Simon. "Interview: Elton Cox and Edward Blankenheim Discuss the 1961 Freedom Ride." *Weekend Edition*, NPR, Saturday, April 7, 2001.
30. Quoted in Cozzens. "Freedom Rides."

Chapter Three: The Ride Gets Bumpy

31. Halberstam. *The Children*, p. 251.
32. Quoted in Halberstam. *The Children*, p. 261.
33. Quoted in Simon. "Interview."
34. Lewis. *Walking with the Wind*, p. 140.
35. Quoted in *American Experience*. "Freedom Riders."
36. Quoted in *The Oprah Winfrey Show*. "Oprah Honors Freedom Riders."
37. Taylor Branch. *Parting the Waters: America in the King Years, 1954–1963*. New York: Simon and Schuster, 1988, p. 418.
38. Boyd. *We Shall Overcome*, p. 92.
39. "Fred Shuttlesworth: He Pushed Martin Luther King, Jr. into Greatness." *Journal of Blacks in Higher Education*, October 31, 2001.
40. Quoted in *American Experience*. "Freedom Riders."
41. Quoted in Arsenault. *Freedom Riders*, p. 136.
42. Quoted in Arsenault. *Freedom Riders*, p. 154.
43. Quoted in Wexler. *The Civil Rights Movement*, p. 129.

44. Quoted in Lewis. *Walking with the Wind*, p. 143.
45. Quoted in Wexler. *The Civil Rights Movement*, p. 130.
46. Halberstam. *The Children*, p. 265.
47. Quoted in Wexler. *The Civil Rights Movement*, p. 133.
48. Scott Sines. "A Bumpy Ride to Freedom." *Spokane (WA) Spokesman Review*, February 18, 2001.
49. Todd Moye. "Freedom Riders: 1961 and the Struggle for Racial Justice." *Journal of Southern History*, August 1, 2007.

Chapter Four: The Ride Continues: Montgomery, Alabama

50. Quoted in Hampton and Fayer. *Voices of Freedom*, p. 82.
51. Quoted in Williams. *Eyes on the Prize*, p. 149.
52. Quoted in CBS Atlanta. "Congressman Lewis Joins Elite Group." February 15, 2011. http://atlanta.cbslocal.com/2011/02/15/congressman-lewis-joins-elite-group.
53. Quoted in *American Experience*. "Freedom Riders."
54. Moye. "Freedom Riders."
55. Quoted in David Halberstam, ed. *Defining a Nation: Our America and the Source of Its Strength*. Washington, DC: National Geographic, 2003, p. 183.
56. Quoted in Halberstam. *Defining a Nation*, p. 183.
57. Quoted in *American Experience*. "Freedom Riders."
58. Quoted in Halberstam. *The Children*, p. 306.
59. Quoted in Nathan Turner Jr. "Freedom Rides of 1961 in Alabama." *Birmingham News*, May 1, 2011.
60. Quoted in Hampton and Fayer. *Voices of Freedom*, pp. 86–87.
61. Derek Charles Catsam. "Mister This Is Not Your Fight: The 1961 Montgomery Freedom Ride Riots." *Studies in Literary Imagination*, September 22, 2007.
62. Quoted in Lewis. *Walking with the Wind*, p. 155.
63. Quoted in Arsenault. *Freedom Riders*, p. 214.
64. Quoted in Wexler. *The Civil Rights Movement*, p. 118.
65. Quoted in Halberstam. *The Children*, p. 321.
66. Quoted in Halberstam. *The Children*, p. 304.
67. Quoted in Arsenault. *Freedom Riders*, p. 215.
68. Quoted in Arsenault. *Freedom Riders*, p. 219.
69. Quoted in Arsenault. *Freedom Riders*, p. 220.
70. Quoted in Branch. *Parting the Waters*, p. 450.
71. Halberstam. *The Children*, p. 318.
72. Branch. *Parting the Waters*, p. 434.
73. Arsenault. *Freedom Riders*, p. 221.
74. Lewis. *Walking with the Wind*, p. 161.
75. Quoted in Diane Tennant. "A Pioneer Reflects on History: James

Farmer Describes Triumphs, Missed Opportunities." *Virginian-Pilot* (Norfolk, VA), January 17, 1999.

Chapter Five: The Arrests

76. Quoted in Hampton and Fayer. *Voices of Freedom*, p. 92.
77. Quoted in Lewis. *Walking with the Wind*, p. 166.
78. Arsenault. *Freedom Riders*, p. 257.
79. Quoted in Hampton and Fayer. *Voices of Freedom*, p. 94.
80. Quoted in *American Experience*. "Freedom Rides."
81. Lewis. *Walking with the Wind*, p. 169.
82. Quoted in Arsenault. *Freedom Riders*, p. 355.
83. Quoted in Civil Rights Movements Veterans. "Civil Rights Movement Timeline, 1961." www.crmvet.org/tim/timhis61.htm#1961frides.
84. Quoted in Civil Rights Movements Veterans. "Civil Rights Movement Timeline, 1961."
85. Quoted in Etheridge et al. *Breach of Peace*, p. 122.
86. Quoted in Hampton and Fayer. *Voices of Freedom*, p. 96.
87. Quoted in Arsenault. *Freedom Riders*, p. 338.

Chapter Six: Impact and Reflections

88. Quoted in Wexler. *The Civil Rights Movement*, p. 133.
89. Quoted in Arsenault. *Freedom Riders*, p. 439.
90. Arsenault. *Freedom Riders*, p. 462.
91. Quoted in Wexler. *The Civil Rights Movement*, p. 119.
92. Quoted in Boyd. *We Shall Overcome*, p. 98.
93. Halberstam. *The Children*, p. 396.
94. Quoted in Martin. "Freedom Riders Reflect on 50th Anniversary."
95. *Jet*. "Fortieth Anniversary of Freedom Rides Celebrated with Special Bus Trip." May 28, 2001.
96. Lewis. *Walking with the Wind*, p. 175.
97. Quoted in Arsenault. *Freedom Riders*, p. 511.
98. Quoted in Cozzens. "Freedom Rides."
99. Quoted in *American Experience*. "Freedom Riders."
100. Halberstam. *The Children*, p. 433.
101. Quoted in Etheridge et al. *Breach of Peace*, p. 203.
102. Quoted in Civil Rights Movements Veterans. "Civil Rights Movement Timeline, 1961."
103. Lewis. *Walking with the Wind*, p. 81.
104. Arsenault. *Freedom Riders*, p. 512.
105. Quoted in Etheridge et al. *Breach of Peace*, p. 46.

Glossary

boycott: An instance of people joining together to abstain from doing something.

Cold War: An intense political and military rivalry; in this case between the United States and the Union of Soviet Socialist Republics.

Communist: A follower of communism, a political doctrine calling for a violent overthrow of capitalism and the creation of a classless society.

desegregation: An end to the separation of one race from another.

discrimination: A distinction in favor of one thing or group over another.

integration: The incorporation of a racial group into the whole of society.

lynching: The act of putting someone to death, usually by hanging, through mob action.

pacifist: Someone who is opposed to war and violence.

racism: The belief that there are inherent differences between the races and that one race is superior to the others.

radical: A person who holds extreme beliefs.

segregation: The separation of one racial group from another.

For More Information

Books

Linda Jacobs Altman. *The American Civil Rights Movement: The African American Struggle for Equality.* Berkeley Heights, NJ: Enslow, 2004. The author presents an overall look at the civil rights movement.

Ann Bausum. *Freedom Riders: John Lewis and Jim Zwerg on the Front Lines of the Civil Rights Movement.* Washington, DC: National Geographic, 2006. This book focuses on the Freedom Rides from the beginning to the end and centers on two remarkable individuals, one black, one white, who participated in the rides.

Sheila Hardy and P. Stephen Hardy. *Extraordinary People of the Civil Rights Movement.* New York: Scholastic, 2007. This book has a section on the Freedom Rides and includes biographies of a number of prominent civil rights leaders.

James Haskins. *Bayard Rustin: Behind the Scenes of the Civil Rights Movement.* New York: Hyperion, 1997. A biography of a key civil rights leader who was a believer in nonviolence and helped steer the movement in that direction.

Deborah Kent. *The Story of the Freedom Riders.* Chicago: Children's Press, 1993. An overview of the Freedom Rides.

Casey King and Linda Barrett Osborne. *Oh, Freedom! Kids Talk About the Civil Rights Movement with the People Who Made It Happen.* New York: Knopf, 1997. A series of interviews with the people who made an impact in the civil rights movement.

Robert H. Mayer. *When the Children Marched.* Berkeley Heights, NJ: Enslow, 2008. A book highlighting the Birmingham, Alabama, civil rights movement, which includes a section on the Freedom Riders.

Diane McWhorter. *A Dream of Freedom: The Civil Rights Movement from 1954 to 1968.* New York: Scholastic, 2004. A book about the civil rights movement with a chapter about the Freedom Rides.

Fred Powledge. *We Shall Overcome: Heroes of the Civil Rights Movement.* New York: Charles Scribner's Sons, 1993. Focusing on the thousands of people who participated in the civil rights movement, the author presents an overview of the movement.

Time-Life Editors. *Turbulent Years: The 60s.* Richmond, VA: Time-Life,

1998. This book has a small section on the Freedom Rides.

Mary C. Turck. *Freedom Song: Young Voices and the Struggle for Civil Rights*. Chicago: Chicago Review, 2009. This book presents an overview of the civil rights era and includes a CD featuring many of the songs of the time.

Periodicals

Clayborne Carson. "Student Nonviolent Coordinating Committee." In *Encyclopedia of African American Culture and History*, edited by Colin A. Palmer. New York: Macmillan Reference USA, 2006.

Emily Claypool. "Doing the Right Things." *Cobblestone*, April 1, 2008.

"James Farmer." In *Encyclopedia of World Biography*, 2004.

Marcia Amidon Lusted. "One Way Ticket to New Orleans, Please: Freedom Riders of 1961." *Cobblestone*, April 1, 2008.

Public Radio

Terry Gross. "Get on the Bus: The Freedom Riders of 1961." National Public Radio, January 12, 2006. www.npr.org/templates/story/story .php?storyId=5149667.

Renee Montagne. "The Reverend James Lawson: An Advocate of Peaceful Change." *Morning Edition*, NPR, December 26, 2006. www.npr.org/ templates/story/story.php?story ID=6676164.

Internet Sources

Susan Eckelmann. "Freedom Rides." Encyclopedia of Alabama, July 24, 2008. www.encyclopediaofalabama .org/face/ArticlePrintable.jsp?id=h-1 605.

Black Past.org. "*Morgan v. Virginia* (1946)." www.blackpast.org/? q=primary/mor gan-v-virginia- 1946.

Websites

Bull Connor, History Learning Site (www.historylearningsite.co.uk/bull _connor.htm). This site offers a biography of Alabama's Bull Connor, who played a significant role in the Freedom Rides.

Civil Rights Movement Veterans (http://crmvet.org). This website covers the history of the civil rights movement.

Gandhi on Nonviolence (http://sfr-21 .org/gandhi-nonviolence.html). This site discusses Mohandas Gandhi's stance on nonviolence.

The History of CORE, Congress of Racial Equality (www.core-online .org/History/history.htm). This site provides a look at the history of this organization from beginning to present day.

National Association for the Advancement of Colored People (www.naacp.org). This website is the home of the civil rights organization.

SNCC 50th Anniversary Conference (www.sncc50thanniversary.org/sncc.html). This site commemorates the 1960 founding of the Student Nonviolent Coordinating Committee at Shaw University in Raleigh, North Carolina.

Southern Christian Leadership Conference (www.sclcnational.org/content/sclc/splash.htm). This website features the history of the Southern Christian Leadership Conference.

Index

A

Africa, 27

Alabama Christian Movement for Human Rights, 46

Anniston (AL) bus bombing (1961), 6–7, 44–45, *45*, 96

Arsenault, Raymond, 65, 88, 98

B

Baker, Ray Stannard, 14

Barbeem, William, 60

Bergman, Walter, 47, 89

Blair, Ezell, Jr., 27

Blankenhein, Edward, 44

Bloody Sunday (Selma, AL, 1965), 89

Board of Education of Topeka, Kansas, Brown v. (1954), 21–22, 37–38

Bond, Julian, 47

Boynton, Bruce, 34–35

Boynton v. Virginia (1960), 6, 34–35, 81

Branch, Taylor, 45, 47, 65

Brinkley, David, 80

Browder v. Gayle (1956), 24

Brown, Henry Billings, 12

Brown, Linda, 22

Brown v. Board of Education of Topeka, Kansas (1954), 21–22, 37–38

Burks-Brooks, Catherine, 59

C

Carawan, Guy, 34

Carey, Gordon, 35

Carmichael, Stokley, 76, 90, *90*

Catsam, Derek Charles, 60

Civil Rights Act (1964), 62, 91, 94
  signing of, *95*

Civil rights movement
  anthem of, 34
  impact of Freedom Rides on, 8–9, 90, 96, 98
  role of media in, 52

Clinton, Bill, 17

Coffin, William Sloane, Jr., 81

Collins, Lucretia, 60

Commission on Civil Rights, U.S., 26

Congress of Racial Equality (CORE), 14, 17, 18, 25, 88
  end of Freedom Rides and, 52–53
  financial burdens on, 78–80

Connor, Eugene "Bull," 47, 48, 50, *50, 56, 58*

Cook, Tom, 47

CORE. *See* Congress of Racial Equality

Cowling, E.L., 43

Cox, B. Elton, 38

Cox, Benjamin, 38

Cozzens, Lisa, 21, 27

D

Department of Justice, U.S., 94
  segregation challenged by, 86–88

Desegregation
  of public schools, 22
  of public transportation, 86–89

Doar, John, 61–62

Duckworth, Roman, 88

Picture Credits

Cover: Paul Schutzer/Time & Life Pictures/Getty Images
AFP/AFP/Getty Images, 95
Anthony Potter Collection/Getty Images, 16
AP Images, 11, 53, 77, 82
AP Images/str, 45
AP Images/The Free-Lance Star, Peter Cihelka, 92
AP Images/The Herald, Andy Burris, 97
AP Images/William A. Smith, 50
© Bettmann/Corbis, 13, 26, 31, 43, 49, 57, 61, 64, 74, 87
Buyenlarge/Getty Images, 19
Donald Uhrbrock/Time & Life Pictures/Getty Images, 33, 58
Don Cravens/Time & Life Pictures/Getty Images, 23, 46
© Flip Schulke/Corbis, 90
Hulton Archive/Getty Images, 20
© Jack Moebes/Corbis, 29
Joseph Scherschel/Time & Life Pictures/Getty Images, 67
Lee Lockwood/Time & Life Pictures/Getty Images, 39, 79
Leigh Vogel/Getty Images, 91
Lynn Pelham/Time & Life Pictures/Getty Images, 17
Paul Schutzer/Time & Life Pictures/Getty Images, 8, 36, 69, 72–73

About the Author

Anne Wallace Sharp is the author of the adult book *Gifts*; several children's books, including *Daring Pirate Women*; and eighteen other titles for Lucent Books. She has also written numerous magazine articles for both adults and juveniles. A retired registered nurse, Sharp has a degree in history. Her interests include reading, traveling, and spending time with her two grandchildren, Jacob and Nicole. Sharp lives in Beavercreek, Ohio.